CW01429772

'TASTES,

thoughts on South African cuisine

Hilary Biller and John Peacock

'TASTES'

thoughts on South African cuisine

Thanks to all the food personalities in the book for your time, effort and enthusiasm – it made putting Tastes together such a pleasure.

Thanks also to Diane Peacock for all her hard work and support.

ZEBRA

First published by Zebra Press, an imprint of Southern Books
(a division of the New Holland Struik Publishing Group (Pty) Ltd.)
PO Box 3103, Halfway House, 1685, South Africa
Tel: (011) 315-3633
Fax: (011) 315-3810
Email: zebrastaff@icelogic.co.za

First edition 1998
© in text, Hilary Biller
© in photographs, John Peacock

All rights reserved. No part of this publication may be reproduced, stored in a retrieval system or transmitted, in any form or by any means, electronic, mechanical, photocopying, recording or otherwise, without the prior written permission of the copyright holder(s).

ISBN 1 86872 247 3

Designer: John Peacock
Cover design: Micha McKerr

Set in Caslon 540 Roman 12/15
Reproduction by: Positive Proof, Randburg
Printed and bound by: Colorgraphic, Durban

Plates for Heinz Brunner: Villeroy & Boch
Plates for Wilfred Coelho and Uday Salunkhe: The Crockery Warehouse
Plate for front cover: The Crockery Warehouse

Colour photographs shot on Agfachrome supplied by Milton Lavenski Photographic
Film processing by Beith Digital
Scanning by Beith Digital

African gingerbeer

South African cooks have, until very recently, been given short shrift internationally. It is only in the last few years that there has been recognition of the wonderful idiosyncracies of local food and the communities from which it is drawn – from boboties and bredies to vetkoek, from butternut soup to mopani worms, from an exquisitely braised breast of ostrich to pumpkin fritters sparkling with cinnamon sugar. And from Malays and Afrikaners, from Indians and Italians, from Zulus and from the English – all of them South Africans.

What we are in the process of creating, as the country climbs out of its past and enters its future, is a South African cuisine as diverse as that of the United States and infinitely more interesting than that of Australia. That diversity is lavishly featured in this superbly compiled and illustrated book. Here we have the wonderful Cass Abrahams rejoicing in the subtleties of Cape Malay cooking; here that stalwart of the South African cooking scene, Billy Gallagher, delights with contemporary offerings; here some of the secrets, redolent with the perfume of home-grown basil and statuesquely reduced sauces from the

ord

renowned kitchens of the former Cybele Forest Lodge cooks, are revealed.

All this, and more, on these beautifully filled pages. You can almost smell the food, touch the texture of summer-ripened figs, lick the sauce off a plate. John Peacock's food photography is almost spare: the food is allowed to speak for itself, and it does, magnificently and sometimes voluptuously. And food writer and cook Hilary Biller's skilled hand is clearly visible in the subject matter and in the passion with which she has attacked her task and coaxed some superlative recipes out of passionate cooks, each of them reflecting, in their varied ways, the varied food from the people of the south.

Tastes is all about the passion for food and the passion of the people who cook it. It's been said that when all other senses fail, the sense of taste remains, that final, satisfying pleasure. With this book in hand – what a way to go.

Jenny Crwys-Williams
Johannesburg
October 1998

Con...

ents

Introdu

As a nation, South Africans boast of excellent sports teams, we speak highly of our wine industry, but we have never promoted our food culture with the same sense of pride. Even the simple question of what true South African cuisine is, evokes diverse responses. In our search to find the answer to this question, we discovered that South African food is an exciting fusion of tastes, textures and cultures. 'Fusion' is a trendy, descriptive food-word that refers to the blending of culturally different cuisines. It is the idea of fusion that was the foundation of *Tastes*.

For photographer extraordinaire, John Peacock, and food writer, Hilary Biller, contact with a whole host of food personalities from food editors to top chefs, food stylists, and cookbook authors initiated this tribute to our emerging multi-faceted cuisine.

By combining the written word with unique photographic interpretation, we have attempted to document the diverse elements that make up South African cuisine – a cuisine we believe is on the brink of a rebirth. It is a cuisine formed by settlers and visitors alike, where exotic flavours have intertwined with local food and customs in a fluid and ever-changing marriage of tastes.

Numerous food personalities have moulded the way South Africans are eating. On the following pages we present some of those people, all of whom are vital links in the chain of influence that is shaping what South African food is and what it will become.

Hilary Biller and John Peacock
Johannesburg
September 1998

'

What I enjoy most about food is that it connects families and people in a more meaningful way. It is nurturing, comforting and sustaining. Food has become the vital link in keeping us together. I am absolutely passionate about food ... the way it looks, the way it tastes, the combination of flavours and most of all the way it brings us together.

Hilary Biller

It's the visual interpretation of the recipe that awakens the appetite and that gastronomic drama that people call taste. The simplest, most common of foods has an infinite repertoire of potential imagery.

John Peacock

,

'

When Muslims invite guests round, they express a *niyyat*, or intention to have a feast. After these feasts people are often seen to wrap left-overs in serviettes to take home with them. This is not considered impolite, for once the *niyyat* is made, the food no longer belongs to the hosts, but to the guests whom they intended to entertain.

,

Cass Abrahams

ahams

Cass Abrahams is a name synonymous with true Cape Malay flavours and culture. Gauteng born and a teacher by training, Cass married a Muslim and embraced the Cape Flats, in the centre of the Cape Malay community, as home. Her natural interest in food prompted her to join the Tastic Rice Corporation many years ago as an in-store promoter. Today she is their national food consultant.

Marriage made Cass realise that cooking was a priority. As a novice she quickly learnt the skill by stealing with her eyes! Her inspired creation of true Cape Malay flavour, with a unique blend of spices, led to the founding of her spice company, Cass Abrahams' Cape Malay Spices. Today the company exports this special flavour throughout the world.

Consulting for restaurants, hotels and lodges, and catering for private dinner parties and large international functions, both locally and overseas, has gained Cass much acclaim. She is determined to educate people about the enchantment conveyed by the Cape's wonderful food. *The Culture and Cuisine of the Cape Malays* is her first cookbook.

The intimate blending of flavours is the soul of Cape Malay cuisine. Each spice is balanced with another, yin and yang, sweet and sour.

masala fish

Masala fish falls into the 'huiskos' category – it is traditionally regarded as everyday food on the Cape Malay table. This tasty fish dish, marinated in a mixture of aromatic spices, is usually served with rice.

Serves 6–8

30ml coriander seeds
30ml cumin seeds
10 garlic cloves
2 green chillies
10ml salt
15ml masala
5ml turmeric
1kg snoek or firm-fleshed fish, cut into portions
vegetable oil for frying
juice of 3 lemons
3 medium tomatoes

Pound coriander seeds, cumin seeds, garlic, chillies and salt together. (If a food processor or blender is used then add garlic cloves while the blade is running. This prevents the cloves sticking under the blades.)
Add masala and turmeric to form a thick paste. Rub paste into fish portions and leave for 15 minutes. Heat the oil and fry fish for 8–10 minutes on each side until cooked.
Remove from pan, arrange on a serving platter and sprinkle with lemon juice.
Cut tomatoes into thick slices and fry in the same oil for 2 minutes. Layer on top of the fish. Serve with rice and sambals.

> *Curries, bredies and soet patats were once looked down upon as the food of the slaves of the Cape.*

vegetable curry

This is a more modern, healthier alternative to the fatty curries prepared with mutton or lamb that many South Africans expect from a Malay cook.

Serves 6

30ml vegetable oil
1 large onion, chopped
1 stick cassia
5ml cumin seeds
2 cardamom pods
1 large tomato, chopped
1kg mixed vegetables, peeled and chopped
5ml ginger and garlic paste
2ml turmeric
5ml ground cumin
5ml ground coriander
5ml masala
salt to taste

Heat the oil in a large saucepan. Fry onion, cassia, cumin and cardamom pods until the onions are soft.
Add the tomato and the rest of the ingredients and stir well. Braise on a moderate heat until the vegetables are cooked but not mushy.
Serve with roti (Indian flat breads) and chutney or a selection of sambals.

'

Afrikaans food is no different to Cape Malay food. The slaves made the same cookies that the white women made. The only difference was in the name, hers were called Hertzoggies!

,

pumpkin bredie

Bredie is an old Cape Malay name for a dish of meat and vegetables stewed together so that the flavours intermingle. Bredies are extremely popular on the Cape Malay table, and form the bulk of 'huiskos'. A cook's skill is truly tested when making a good bredie. There is a narrow margin between perfection and overcooking. It is best to use the flat, white pumpkin or even butternut in this dish, as the flesh remains firm when cooked and does not become watery.

Serves 6

250ml water
2 large onions, chopped
3 whole allspice
4 cloves
45ml oil
1kg chopped mutton
4 cloves garlic, crushed
4 sticks cinnamon
5cm piece root ginger, crushed
2kg pumpkin, peeled and cubed
45ml butter
30ml brown sugar
salt
freshly ground pepper to taste
chopped chives for garnishing

Place the water in a large saucepan and bring to the boil. Add the onions, allspice and cloves. Simmer until all the water has been absorbed. Add oil and sauté until the onions are golden. Add the mutton, garlic, cinnamon and ginger, then braise over a medium heat until the meat is a rich brown colour and is almost done.
Add the pumpkin pieces and stir, making sure the meat and pumpkin are well combined. Cover the saucepan with a tight-fitting lid and allow the bredie to simmer until the pumpkin is soft and mushy. The meat must be falling off the bone.
Add butter, brown sugar and seasoning to taste. Garnish with chopped chives and serve with rice.

> *Cape Malay cooking deserves to be placed on the map like Cajun food. When it is, I know I can close my eyes and die happy.*

boeber

A warm and comforting pudding, made with milk and flavoured with nuts and spices. Traditionally made for friends and family members who are sad or depressed, boeber would be the ideal solace for a daughter who had just broken off a special relationship. This pudding is also made on the fifteenth day of the Muslim fast, and sent to one's neighbours to celelebrate.

Serves 6

100g butter
250ml lokshen*
2 sticks cinnamon
2 cardamom pods
1 litre milk
40g sago, soaked in milk
sugar to taste
10ml rosewater
150g sultanas
100g flaked almonds
ground cinnamon

Melt the butter in a saucepan. Add lokshen, cinnamon sticks and cardamom pods, then stir over a low heat until the lokshen are golden brown. Add milk and bring to the boil. Cook over a low heat until the lokshen are tender. Add sago and cook, stirring all the time, until the sago is transparent. Stir in sugar, rosewater, sultanas and almonds. Pour into a glass serving bowl. Sprinkle with ground cinnamon and serve warm.

*Lokshen are a type of thin noodle like vermicelli and are available in the pasta section of most supermarkets.

Apartheid alienated people from their cuisine.

Cass Abrahams

Theresa

‘

To identify South African cuisine would be to refer to a
tinned fruit salad ... colourful but nothing standing out,
trapped in a 1960s time warp – the can! Fusion food now
needs to take a look at a north-south combination: the eating
customs of Africa, bringing the family together for long, slow-
cooked, delicious meals, combining the European demand for
quality ... we'd be proud to call this a truly South African cuisine.'

Suzi Holtzhausen

,

Suzi Holtzhausen

Theresa Beukes

Suzi

Beukes

It was the exclusive Cybele Forest Lodge that brought restaurateur Theresa Beukes and chef Suzi Holtzhausen together, in the early 1980s. This was to be the start of a long relationship with food as the anchor. The lodge, well known for its fine cuisine, employed Suzi as executive chef and Theresa for her other passion – gardening.

Theresa Beukes grew up on a farm in the fruit-growing area of Elgin in the Western Cape. A dream of one day owning her own restaurant sustained her through early days of waitressing, cooking and catering, until finally it was fulfilled in the form of her successful Melville restaurant, Sam's Café. Here she has found her niche – her home and her whole life – a true commitment. Here she cooks what she wants, and prides herself on having attracted a clientele who, rather than ordering huge plates of food, prefer starter portion sizes of the highest quality.

Suzi Holtzhausen's first career choice was hotel management – but first she had to learn more about food. Her mentor, Topsi Venter, taught her never to be afraid of experimenting. Working with Topsi and other top food personalities including John Tovey in the Lake District of England gave her invaluable experience. Cybele Lodge and Londolozi Game Lodge established her as a name in African cuisine. Today, as the owner and principal of The Barnes Street Culinary Studio, Suzi operates a full-time cookery school, offers demonstrations and lunches, and is a sought-after caterer. Her one standing appointment each and every Tuesday is as the guest chef at Sam's Café in Melville.

Holtzhausen

> ❛
>
> *I enjoy working as a team — a combined effort of heads and hands. I want to know I have shared what I have learnt. If I learn one new thing each day, it allows me to stay in the food business.*
>
> *Suzi Holtzhausen*
>
> ❜

african orzo risotto

Serves 4

*100g chickpeas, soaked in water overnight and
    drained*
*100g green lentils, soaked in water overnight and
    drained*
15ml sesame seed oil
30ml roasted North African spices
1 onion, finely chopped
2 cloves of garlic, chopped
10ml grated ginger
1 red chilli, chopped
100g orzo (pasta rice)
1 x 410 g can Italian tomatoes, roughly blended
coarse salt & pepper
30ml flat parsley, chopped
Swiss chard, deep-fried
yoghurt
red onions, sliced and deep-fried

North African spices
3 coriander seeds
1 whole clove
1 whole stick cinnamon
2 cumin seeds
2 paprika

Place chickpeas in a pot and cover with filtered water. Simmer until half-cooked and add the lentils. Cook until soft. Strain and wash with filtered water. Set aside.

To make the North African spices, place them on a baking sheet and dry roast for 10 minutes at 190°C. Grind to a powder in a coffee grinder. Heat a clean pot and add the oil. Add spices, onion, garlic, ginger and chilli. Cook through and stir in the orzo. Lower the heat and stir in half the tomato. Simmer to cook the orzo, adding more tomato in small quantities. Stir in the lentils and chickpeas.

Season and stir in the parsley.

Serve on crispy deep-fried Swiss chard or spinach if this is not available, and top with yoghurt and deep fried red onion rings.

> '
> *Hunger is my fascination with food. My earliest and best recollection of food is a sun-warmed, blood-red tomato exploding in my mouth.*
> ,
>   Theresa Beukes

bobotie springrolls with mint chutney

Serves 4

25g butter
30ml olive oil
15ml grated ginger
15ml brown sugar
7ml curry powder mixture
8ml turmeric
5ml salt
2 chives, sliced
500g mince
1 slice white bread, soaked in water and drained
75ml raisins, soaked in port (optional)
25ml chutney
10ml apricot jam
10ml vinegar
10ml Worcester sauce
15 ml tomato sauce
75ml apricots, sliced
100ml almonds, toasted
1 packet springroll pastry *
oil for frying

Garnish
125ml milk
75ml cream
2 eggs

Mint chutney
125ml mint leaves
2 spring onions
5ml crushed garlic
1 green chilli
10ml vinegar
pinch of pepper
salt
2,5ml sugar

Place the first eight ingredients in a heavy-bottomed saucepan and cook slowly for approximately 6 minutes until chives are wilted. Add all the mince ingredients up to and including the almonds and cook on a moderate heat for 10–15 minutes. Allow to cool.
Using two layers of springroll pastry, place 60ml of mince mixture into the centre of each spring roll, fold in the ends and roll up. Preheat oil and fry springrolls until golden brown on all sides. Drain well on absorbent paper.
Combine all the ingredients for the garnish.
Pour into a flat baking sheet. Bake at 160°C until it turns light brown. Remove from the oven, cut into ribbons.
For the mint chutney, place all ingredients up to and including vinegar into food processor and blend. Add salt and sugar to taste. Pour into a bowl.
Serve springrolls hot with garnish and chutney.

* Available at Chinese supermarkets.

20 Tastes: thoughts on South African cuisine

> '
> *It is time for a common goal: understanding our own food heritage and building on the basics is what we should be concerned with.*
>
> *Suzi Holtzhausen*
> ,

seafood pot au feu

Serves 4

4 baby carrots
4 baby leeks
4 celery stalks
750ml filtered water
1 piece lemon zest
250ml chenin blanc white wine
white peppercorns
coarse salt
500g linefish fillets, cut into strips and tied
*   with chives*
4 tiger prawns, deveined
8 fresh mussels, scrubbed and beards removed
4 calamari tubes, cleaned with inner and outer
*   membranes removed*
250g fresh peas, washed and removed from the pods
2,5ml saffron threads
50g unsalted butter

Red pepper mayonnaise
1 red pepper
125ml home-made mayonnaise
salt & pepper

Wash and peel the carrots and leeks and cut them in half lengthways. Cut celery at a slant into strips. Reserve peelings for bouillon. Prepare a court bouillon (poaching liquid for fish) in a poaching pan using water, lemon, wine, peppercorns, coarse salt, and vegetable peelings. Bring to the boil and lower heat to a simmer. Place fish and shellfish into the liquid and simmer covered for 8–10 minutes. Remove fish and seafood with a slotted spoon. Drain and keep warm, covered in a low oven.

Strain the cooking liquid into a saucepan, add vegetables. Set over a medium heat and simmer to reduce by half. Add saffron and heat to infuse the flavour. Adjust the seasoning. Remove vegetables and place in a serving dish with fish and shellfish. Whisk butter into liquid and pour into serving dish.

To make the mayonnaise, place washed and dried red pepper on baking sheet and grill, turning to brown all sides. Remove and cool in plastic bag. Remove skin and seeds and slice. Place in blender with mayonnaise and mix. Season to taste.

Serve drizzled with red pepper mayonnaise, melba toast or toasted buttermilk rusks.

'

The next vogue — back to basics — is to South Africa's advantage. To simplify our dishes, with higher demands for raw quality and simple presentation, will suit our more demanding lifestyles and also allow time for better training for the chefs of the future.

Suzi Holtzhausen

,

roasted caramelised pineapple with vanilla

Serves 4

2 pineapples, peeled and halved lengthways
2,5ml cayenne pepper
15ml fresh ginger, grated
6 vanilla pods
125ml brown sugar

Ginger and pineapple ice cream
4 egg yolks
500 ml cream, whipped until stiff
1/2 x 497g can condensed milk
1/2 pineapple, peeled and blended in food processor
15ml fresh ginger, grated

Place peeled pineapple cut side down on a baking tray. Sprinkle with cayenne pepper and rub ginger onto each piece. Spike vanilla pods into pineapple. Sprinkle with brown sugar and bake at 180°C for 30 minutes or until pineapple is glazed.
To make the ice cream, cream the egg yolks in a mixer. Combine the cream and condensed milk and fold into egg mixture.
Blend together pineapple and ginger and fold into creamed mixture.
Place in a 2,5 litre plastic container with a lid and freeze for 12–14 hours.
Serve with roasted caramelised pineapple.

I spend my time thinking of different ways of combining food. If I can take a traditional dish and make it better, I strive to do it.

Theresa Beukes

Danté, Valeria & Caterina Bollini

Danté and Valeria Bollini grew up in Bologna – the pantry of Italy; home too of the famed Marcella Hazan, whose cookery books have had a great influence on them.

It was tragedy that set the Bollini family on the path of providing locals with a true taste of Italy in the Johannesburg suburb of Oaklands. The untimely death of their son, Filippo, made their lives as accountants difficult to continue. Filippo had often suggested that they open a business that dealt in food, so when Danté (who regularly visited the Italian butchery in the Oaklands Centre) discovered a vacant shop in the centre, the idea took root. The first fresh pasta shop in South Africa – Tortellini D'Oro – was born in 1986. Caterina has since joined her parents and her energy and verve ensure the continuation of this successful enterprise.

'

My grandmother in Italy believed that the way she cooked was the only way – through family recipes and tradition. When my parents and I started in the food business twelve years ago in South Africa, we realised that there was a need to detach from strict traditions in Italian cooking and meet the need of a South African nation whose palate very much appreciated Italian food, but whose tradition often clashed with the way Italian food was prepared. We came up with a simple concept: 'If you are kosher or you don't eat pork, you don't have to add pancetta to pasta fagioli. If you are vegetarian, you can still enjoy a risotto by using vegetable stock instead of a meat stock. And if you are halaal, you can still make a meat sauce by adding spirit vinegar instead of wine. But, *never* deny yourself the pleasures of Italian food!

Caterina Bollini

,

'

Our strong taste memories ensure that we persevere to obtain just the right Italian taste for a particular dish. We will go to any lengths to achieve this. Take the South African tomato – it is very acidic and a poor relative to the Italian tomato. We started off using the local varieties and then tried growing our own, to no avail. We then imported different Italian varieties of seed, which we planted so as to have vine ripened tomatoes, but just could not produce the same taste of those deep red, sweet Italian tomatoes we knew so well. Our compromise is to use Italian canned tomatoes, which we import along with many other Italian specialities in the shop.

Valeria Bollini

,

*Food is such a sensual experience. What's more —
you don't need a partner.*

Danté Bollini

penne peperoni
penne with pepper sauce

Serves 4

2 large peppers, red and yellow
1 large aubergine
1 chilli
100ml olive oil
1 onion, finely chopped
100ml concentrated Italian tomato paste
800g tinned Italian tomatoes
125ml white wine
about 400g imported Italian penne
salt & pepper
parmesan cheese, grated

Slice the peppers in long strips and the aubergine in chunks. Salt the aubergine and allow the excess water and bitterness to drain off for about 45 minutes. Drain and pat dry. Chop the chilli.

Heat the olive oil in a saucepan and sauté the onion until it is translucent. Add the tomato paste, the chilli and the peppers and stir. Add the white wine and allow it to evaporate.

Cook the peppers on a medium heat until they are soft (it will take ½ hour to 45 minutes), adding water if the mixture becomes too dry.

Once the peppers are soft, add the aubergines and the tomatoes with their juices, then cook for a further 45 minutes until the sauce thickens, stirring occasionally. Season with salt and pepper.

Once the sauce is ready, throw the pasta into a large pot of boiling, salted water. Cook the pasta until al dente, strain through a sieve and dress with the sauce. Serve hot with a good grating of parmesan cheese.

verdure grigliate
grilled vegetables

Serves 6

grilled peppers

6 peppers
100ml Italian extra virgin olive oil
60ml parsley, chopped with 1–2 garlic cloves
3 anchovy fillets, chopped (optional)
30ml baby capers, chopped (optional)
salt & pepper

Wash the peppers well under running water and dry them on a kitchen towel.
Place the peppers on a hot grill or in a hot oven at 220°C and grill them until the skins swell and separate from the pulp.
Allow the skin to burn slightly on each side of the peppers, turning them from time to time. When the skin has separated completely, remove the peppers from the grill, wrap them in paper and place them in a plastic carrier-bag. Allow them to cool. Peel off the skins and open the peppers, removing the seeds and the inner core. Cut the peeled peppers lengthways into strips and place them in a serving dish. Dress them with olive oil, the parsley garlic, anchovies and capers. Season to taste.
Serve with grilled baby marrows and aubergines.

grilled baby marrows and aubergines

400g fresh baby marrows
3 small aubergines
salt
60ml parsley, chopped with 1–2 garlic cloves
1 tablespoon dried oregano
100ml extra virgin olive oil
salt & pepper

Slice the baby marrows and aubergines thinly (about 3,5 mm) lengthways, using a sharp knife, and place them on a serving dish. Sprinkle them freely with salt and allow the excess water and bitterness to drain for about 45 minutes.
Drain and pat dry with a kitchen towel.
Heat a grilling pan and grill the vegetables on each side until charred stripes appear across them.
As you place the vegetables on a serving dish, dress them with the chopped parsley and garlic, oregano, olive oil, salt and a good grating of black pepper. Serve at room temperature with grilled peppers.

> '
> The combination of a savoury flavour and a sweet one is more common to a South African cuisine than to an Italian one.
>
> *Caterina Bollini*
>
> '

tortellini di zucca con panna e salvia

butternut tortellini with cream and sage sauce

This recipe is not the most common in Italy, but South Africans just love butternut! The addition of amaretti biscuits (Italian almond macaroon) and almonds to this recipe gives the filling a nutty flavour. The making of the pasta shape takes practice: it took me six months of training in my grandmother's kitchen (I was 10 years old) before I could successfully make the perfect tortellino shape. The halfmoon shape (mezza luna) as illustrated is easier to make.

Serves 6

400g baked butternut pulp
200g ricotta cheese
100g parmesan cheese, freshly grated
1 large egg
10 amaretti biscuits, crushed to powder
20 almonds, peeled and chopped
salt & pepper
500g basic pasta dough

Cream & sage sauce:
50g butter
1 sprig sage
500ml fresh cream
salt & pepper
dash of ground nutmeg

Combine butternut, ricotta cheese, parmesan cheese, egg, amaretti biscuits and almonds in a mixing bowl. Mix until well blended. Season with salt and pepper.

Once you have made the basic pasta dough, pass the dough through a pasta machine, then place spoonfuls of filling in the centre at 5cm distances.

Fold the dough over and squash it around the edges to form a parcel. Cut the shape of a half moon around each piece of filling. Repeat until all the filling is used up.

To make the sauce, melt the butter in a saucepan and fry the sage lightly. Add cream, salt, pepper and nutmeg.

Boil the tortellini in abundant salted water until tender. Drain and dress with the sauce.

Serve hot with more parmesan cheese.

'

Tagliatelle with ragu is a typical dish from Bologna, not to be con-fused with the South African staple, spaghetti bolognaise.

Caterina Bollini

,

tagliatelle con ragu alla bolognaise
tagliatelle with bolognaise sauce

It takes time and love to prepare this dish. The sauce should cook slowly for about 2–3 hours and should be stirred often for the proper blending of ingredients to take place. Tagliatelle are the traditional accompaniment.

Serves 4

30ml olive oil
30g butter
1 onion, chopped
1 stick celery, chopped
1 carrot, peeled and chopped
300g lean beef mince and 300g pork mince
or
600g beef mince
125ml dry white wine
1 x 400g can Italian plum tomatoes
125ml milk (optional)
salt & pepper
350g tagliatelle
parmesan cheese, grated

Heat the olive oil and butter in a deep, heavy casserole and sauté the onion, celery and carrot, until the onion becomes transluscent. Add the mince and brown.
Add the white wine and stir occasionally until the wine has evaporated.
Chop the tomatoes and add to the sauce with their juices. Bring to a steady simmer, stirring occasionally, adding milk if used.
Allow the sauce to reduce over a low heat for about 2½ to 3 hours, stirring occasionally. Season to taste.
When the sauce is ready, boil the tagliatelle in a large pot with abundant salted water for about 4 minutes for homemade pasta or according to package instructions for bought pasta. Strain. Serve hot with sauce and a generous helping of grated parmesan cheese.

‘ *My mother, not a rich woman, but a wonderful cook, said she had nothing to leave me but the inheritance of her passion for food.*

Valeria Bollini ,

Heinz Br

'A recipe is an inspiration. I believe that you should read recipes and then adapt them to what you feel like. Often the simplest dishes are the most tasty. Many people try too hard when creating a dish or a meal. Imagine a freshly caught fish, taken home or better still eaten fresh on the beach, gutted then prepared with some lemon juice, sea salt, some fresh vegetables such as leek, celery, onions, carrots and some fresh dill and thyme, a touch of white wine, then wrapped in aluminum foil and slowly cooked over a coal fire. This is a heavenly dish and so easy to make. Why spoil it with a lot of other unnecessary ingredients? That's why I believe that simplicity and taste are the art of cooking. It is very difficult to go wrong with prawns or lobster, but to prepare a really tasty oxtail with a good flavour and texture is what cooking is all about.'

Heinz Brunner

A Swiss national, Heinz Brunner grew up with a passion for food, instilled in him by his father, a butcher. At the age of 13 he found himself in France, studying French in the mornings and spending the afternoons in a French kitchen. By 17 he had completed a two-and-a-half year apprenticeship in Zurich and was ready to conquer the world. After various jobs, including two seasons in Arosa, Heinz arrived at The Carlton, which was one of the top hotels in South Africa at that time. With a staff of 1100 and a kitchen staff of 120, half of whom were European – German, Swiss or Austrian – it was a city in itself.

A career that has spanned many years has taken him from The Carlton, to executive chef of a number of establishments, namely the new Sandton Holiday Inn, the Wynford Club, followed by First National Bank. It was here that Brunner had his first exposure to management. At First National Bank he changed from a chef's jacket to a suit and tie and became involved in the design of Bank City, travelling around South Africa to oversee all the in-house catering and executive dining rooms.

Today, as the Development Director of Compass South Africa, Brunner has brought more than his Swiss perfection to the table. He has been actively involved with the Chefs Association since 1979 and it is this body that has seen the chefs' status uplifted. He is vice-president of the World Association of Cooks. In this role, he has improved standards of South African food and carried the flag of South African cuisine worldwide.

'

For me, to have cooked and served a well-prepared dish and to see my guests enjoying themselves is the applause for an artist after a great performance.

,

sweet potato-morogo lasagne

Serves 4

4 medium sweet potatoes, cooked
30ml olive oil
10g garlic, chopped
10g onions, finely chopped
200g morogo*, blanched
pinch nutmeg
salt & ground black pepper, to taste
2 egg yolks
200ml milk
8 basil leaves
80g pesto
100ml tomato & basil sauce
12 pine nut kernels for garnish

Peel the sweet potatoes and slice finely into about 2–3 mm thick slices.
Heat olive oil to a medium heat in a frying pan. Add garlic and onions and sauté until transparent.
Add morogo and sauté. Season with nutmeg, salt and black pepper.
Beat egg yolks together in a separate dish, then add the milk.
Grease 6 ramekin dishes. Place about 5 slices of potato into each. Spoon morogo over potato to about 1cm thick.
Arrange another layer of potatoes, followed by a second layer of morogo. Finish with a final layer of potatoes. Pour the egg and milk mixture into each dish.
Poach in a bain-marie in a medium oven at 180°C for about 20 minutes, until egg has set.
Deep fry basil leaves very quickly in hot oil.
Unmould and serve with pesto and tomato and basil sauce, garnished with pine kernels.

* Morogo is a wild spinach-type leaf which grows prolifically in some areas of South Africa. Young spinach or beetroot leaves may be used instead.

A perfect meal is when you have eaten three or four courses and you still have enough space to enjoy some chocolates, a good cognac and a nice cigar.

duo of pasta with Cape goat cheese

Serves 4

200g squid ink pasta
200g chilli pasta
100ml olive oil
seasoning
10g garlic
120g goat cheese marinated in olive oil, cubed
80ml cream
3ml dried origanum
3ml dried thyme
French bread croutons

Boil pastas separately in generous amounts of salted water, until al dente. Cool down under cold water.
Divide the olive oil into three parts and heat two parts in different pots. Heat one kind of pasta in one pot and the other pasta in the other. Season each to taste.
Place the remaining oil in a separate pot, add the goat cheese and sauté quickly (otherwise the cheese melts). Add the cream and herbs, then season to taste.
To serve, twist the squid ink pasta with a fork and arrange on the left-hand side of a plate in a half-moon shape. Arrange the chilli pasta in the same way on the opposite side. Spoon goat cheese mixture in the centre and garnish with French bread croutons.

The worst that can happen to me is an overloaded, unappetising plate of food. Food must say 'eat me'.

ostrich medallions Kalahari

I enjoy using different local ingredients. The Kalahari truffle, similar to the French truffle in texture but totally different in taste, is one such ingredient. The San have been digging and savouring this underground delicacy for a long time.

Serves 4

12 x 50g ostrich medallions
salt, crushed black pepper
80ml oil
100ml red wine
100ml demi-glace sauce
100ml chicken stock
160g couscous
120g mixture of grilled vegetables, cut into equal
   squares
4 Kalahari truffles*, sliced
12 pieces pear, finely sliced and dried in a moderate
   oven

Season medallions with salt and pepper.
Heat the oil and sauté until they are about medium rare. Set aside in a warm place.
Pour the red wine into the pan and reduce by a third. Then add the demi glace and season to taste. The sauce must not be too thin.
Heat the chicken stock in a saucepan. Add the couscous and cook until done. Season to taste.
Heat the grilled vegetables in an oven.
Sauté the truffles.
To serve, cover half the base of 4 plates with the sauce. Arrange 3 medallions in the sauce on each plate, then the truffles to the right of the meat. Scoop couscous onto the other half of each plate in a half-moon shape. Leave a space in each centre for the grilled vegetables. Garnish with pear slices.

* Kalahari truffles are found in Namibia. They are seasonal and are available from certain speciality stores.

It is important in cooking to use good colours as well as properly cooked food.

Natal crocodile with mealie and polenta cake

Serves 4

300g deboned crocodile*, sliced
50ml olive oil
salt and ground pepper
30g flour
seasoning
5–10ml curry powder
100ml white wine
200ml chicken stock
200g mealie meal
200g polenta
100g sundried tomatoes, chopped
80g butter
4 baby marrows, cut into ribbons
40g fried onions

Season crocodile and dust with flour. Heat olive oil over a moderate heat.
Sauté crocodile in the oil, then add curry powder and white wine and cook for 3-5 minutes.
Remove crocodile and set aside. Boil the wine until it reduces, then add some of the stock.
Return crocodile to pan and set aside.
Cook the mealie meal and polenta separately, then allow them to cool slightly.
Spread half the mealie meal about 1cm thick, along the base of a long, greased dish. Top with half the polenta (also 1cm thick). Then spread a fine layer of sundried tomatoes, followed by the remaining mealie meal and polenta. Leave to set
Cut half-moon shapes out of the polenta and mealie meal cake. Fry in butter and season.
To serve, arrange 2 half-moons on the centre of each plate, leaving the centre open. Spoon crocodile mixture in each centre. Garnish with baby marrows and fried onions.

* Available from speciality butcheries.

To me a good meal, some great wine and enjoyable company are the height of enjoyment.

granadilla mille-feuille

Serves 4

125ml granadilla pulp
250ml cream, whipped
12g powdered gelatine (or 2 leaves)
45ml warm water
30ml Amarula liqueur
80g canned or fresh mango slices
150g dark chocolate for coating
150g white chocolate for coating
8 strawberries for garnishing
cooked pastry twirl for decoration

Fold granadilla pulp into cream.
Dissolve gelatine in lukewarm water. If you are using leaves, then squeeze out excess water.
Add gelatine and Amarula to granadilla mixture and gently combine all the ingredients. Leave mousse to set in a suitable glass dish that is not too deep.
Cut mango slices into chunks, place in a blender and liquidise to a thick, but not runny, coulis. If the coulis is too thick, add some of the mango liquid.
Melt the chocolates separately. Do not allow the chocolate to become too hot: it will turn grey in colour. Pour onto a flat surface and allow to set. Lift the chocolate with a spatula and break it into pieces about 8–10 cm in length. You will need about 2–3 pieces of each colour.
Slice the strawberries and dry out in a moderate oven.
To serve, place 1 piece of white and 1 piece of brown chocolate at the outer edge of each plate. Place a quenelle of granadilla mousse on each chocolate piece, followed by another piece of chocolate on top of that. Spoon mango coulis in front of each quenelle. Garnish with strawberry slices. A pastry twirl adds the final touch.

'

*Creativity in cooking lies in the interpreta-
tion of the recipe.*

Heinz Brunner

'

'

We are teaching South Africans to eat curries. They have moved away from merely ordering lamb, fish, chicken or vegetable curry, and from the fiery Durban interpretation. Curry means sauce, not hot! Working with authentic Tandoor ovens – traditional clay cyclinder-type charcoal ovens with lids – means that we can ensure diners enjoy an authentic Indian culinary experience. We work together like brothers!

With the help of restaurants like the Delhi Palace, South African diners have become more adventurous and interested in Indian cuisine. We've even educated the local Indian community!

Wilfred and Uday Salunkhe

,

Wilfred Coelho

Uday Salunkhe

Pelho

Preparing traditional Indian food – which boasts over 24 different cuisines, all strongly influenced by religion and custom – is a challenge proudly taken on by chefs Coelho and Salunkhe, both of whom served a four-year apprenticeship with the Taj Group in Bombay, specialising in the preparation of North Indian Mogul cuisine.

The Indians who laboured in South Africa's sugar plantations brought with them a food culture that was to have a tremendous impact on palates countrywide. The original Delhi Palace restaurant, situated on the historic site of the hotel in Fordsburg, has long been the home of the finest Indian cuisine, with chefs specially sourced from India for their excellent culinary skills.

Chefs Coelho and Salunkhe have been employed at the Delhi Palace since the group's inception in the late 1980s.

ay Salunkhe

chicken tikka

Serves 4–5

1kg chicken breast fillets
salt to taste
30ml red chilli paste
60ml ginger & garlic paste
60ml cream
50ml lemon juice
50ml butter, melted for basting

Marinade
200ml double thick plain yoghurt
15g garam masala
15ml ginger/garlic paste
20ml lemon juice
50ml oil
15ml red chilli paste
salt to taste

Remove any fat from the chicken breasts and cut them into 3cm pieces.
Mix salt, chilli paste, ginger and garlic paste, cream and lemon juice and rub into the chicken pieces. Set aside for one hour.
To make the marinade, beat the yoghurt in a bowl and combine all the ingredients together. Add chicken to the marinade, cover and leave for 2–3 hours in the refrigerator.
Preheat the oven to 180ºC. Brush a baking tray with melted butter and spread with marinated chicken without overlapping the pieces. Bake for approximately 15 minutes, basting frequently with butter.
Serve as a starter with sliced onions and salad.

tangri kebab

Serves 3–4

12 chicken drumsticks
45ml ginger & garlic paste
15ml crushed black pepper
10g garam masala
15ml green chilli paste
30ml lemon juice
100ml plain yoghurt
1 egg
salt to taste
butter for basting

Skin and clean the drumsticks. Make two deep cuts lengthwise on each drumstick.
Combine all ingredients except the butter and rub into the drumsticks. Set aside for two hours.
Preheat the oven to 160ºC. Rub a baking tray with butter and spread chicken drumsticks on tray. Pour over remaining marinade and bake for 15–30 minutes, basting continuously with melted butter. Serve as a starter on a bed of shredded vegetable salad with chutney.

seekh kebab

Serves 4–5

500g mutton mince
15g garam masala
15ml finely chopped ginger
15ml finely chopped green chillies
15ml finely chopped garlic
1 medium onion, finely chopped
125ml fresh coriander, chopped
5ml fresh mint paste
salt to taste
melted butter for basting

Combine the mince with all the ingredients except melted butter. Mix well and set aside for 15 minutes. Divide into 12 equal portions and roll so each portion is 8–10cm long.
Preheat the oven to 180ºC. Grease a baking tray with melted butter and place kebabs on tray. Bake for 12–15 minutes, basting frequently with melted butter.
Serve with lemon and mint chutney.

Top right, chicken tikka; top left, tangri kebab; bottom left, seekh kebab; bottom right, kastoori kebab (p 58)

A traditional Indian meal comprises many different dishes to be shared and tasted by everyone. South Africans, despite their bigger appetites, are learning not to order just individual portions.

kastoori kebab *(illustrated on p 57)*

Serves 4 – 5

1kg chicken breast fillets
salt to taste
15ml ginger & garlic paste
30ml lemon juice
2,5ml green cardamom powder
50g butter
40ml garam flour (besan)
150ml cream
0,5g saffron, dissolved in a little boiling water
20ml oil
2 eggs
½ bunch fresh coriander, chopped

Clean and cut the chicken fillets into 2,5cm cubes. Rub with salt, ginger and garlic paste, lemon juice and cardamom powder and set aside.
Heat the butter in a pan, add half the garam flour and stir over medium heat until golden brown in colour. Allow to cool.
Place cream, remaining garam flour, saffron, oil, egg yolks and chopped coriander in a bowl. Add chicken and mix well.
Preheat oven to 170°C and roast chicken for 10–12 minutes. Baste with melted butter and bake for 3–5 more minutes.
Serve with chutney and naan.

butter chicken

Serves 4

100g butter
5–6ml green cardamom
2 bay leaves
15ml ginger & garlic paste
1,2kg tomatoes, chopped
200ml water
15ml chilli powder
salt to taste
sugar to taste
125ml cashew nut paste
150ml cream
20 pieces chicken tikka (cooked according to recipe provided on p 56)

Melt half the butter in a heavy-bottomed pan and add the cardamom, bay leaves, ginger and garlic paste and tomatoes. Sauté over low heat for 5–10 minutes. Add water and boil for a further 15 minutes. Once tomatoes are cooked, remove and strain through a fine strainer.
In a separate pan, add tomato pulp, chilli powder, salt and sugar. Bring to the boil. Add cashew nut paste and cook well. Add cream and remaining butter. Add cooked chicken tikkas. Add fresh coriander leaves and serve with rice or naan.

'

We both work with the feel of food — never recipes. This has come with years of experience.

Coelho and Salunkhe

,

navratan korma

Serves 4

100g carrots, peeled and diced
100g cauliflower, broken into small florets
50g French beans, cut into 2cm pieces
50g green peas
100g mushrooms
2 medium potatoes, diced
60ml oil
5ml cumin seeds
2 bay leaves
1 medium onion, chopped
15ml ginger & garlic paste
15ml green chilli paste
100g cashew nut paste
10 raisins
10 whole cashew nuts
100ml cream
salt to taste

Parboil all the vegetables up to and including the potatoes.
In a pan, preheat the oil and add the cumin seeds, bay leaves and onion. Fry till golden brown. Add the ginger and garlic paste, green chilli paste and cashew nut paste. Cook until the ingredients form a definite separation from the gravy. Add remaining ingredients and cook on low heat for 4–5 minutes.
Serve with basmati rice.

Don't ever bluff people with your food. It is your pride. If you have an argument, do not take it out on your food.

Uday Salunkhe

Bill Gallas

'

Our cuisine is evolving, and not yet fully understood. When flying to take up my first job in South Africa in the 1970s, I thought that the food would be very exotic, very spicy, with lots of game. I believed I was coming to the real wild Africa. Instead, when I arrived I discovered quasi-European food with Afrikaner traces and very little African influence.

South African food has changed – the produce has improved so much over the years, the ingredients have become more varied and the willingness on the part of the customer to eat totally different things has seen the cuisine grow and become far more exciting.

,

Bill Gallagher

The name Bill Gallagher is synonomous with South Africa's chefs and cuisine, which Gallagher has been instrumental in bringing into the international arena.

English-born Gallagher began his culinary career as an indentured apprentice chef at the Royal County Hotel in Newcastle, England. He emigrated to South Africa in 1973, joining the Southern Sun Hotel Group as Executive Sous Chef at the Elizabeth Hotel in Port Elizabeth.

An amassed wealth of culinary experience and recognition saw Gallagher on his way to his present position as Group Food & Beverage Director for Southern Sun Hotels. In November 1982 Gallagher was elected Chairman of the South African Chefs Association, a position he still retains. In 1989 he was awarded Honorary Life Presidency. He has represented South Africa in numerous local and international cooking competitions, serving as team captain on several occasions.

In 1995 Gallagher was awarded the degree of Doctor of Culinary Arts by Johnson and Wales University, Miami, Florida. In 1996 at the World Association of Cooks Societies Congress (WACS) in Israel, Gallagher was unanimously elected President of WACS for the term 1996–2000. This is the first time South Africa has had the seat of this presidency – a fitting tribute to one who has done so much for the advancement of South African cuisine.

Food has become much more informal. Our guests are looking not only to eat, but also to be entertained.

North country thick green pea soup

Serves 4

100g onion, chopped
200g leeks, diced
25ml olive oil
50g butter
bouquet garni*
500g frozen green peas
pinch of sugar
800ml chicken stock
pinch of salt
100g smoked hicory ham, diced
5 rashers of bacon, grilled
heart of lettuce, finely shredded
50ml cream

Cook the onion and leeks in the olive oil and butter for a few minutes, then add your bouquet garni, peas and sugar. (Reserve some whole peas for garnish.) Allow to mingle together, add chicken stock, bring to the boil and simmer for 20 minutes. Skim and remove bouquet garni. Place the soup in a blender, purée and strain through a sieve.
Just before serving, reheat and season lightly. While the soup is simmering, add the smoked ham, crisp, bacon rashers cut into 1cm pieces, finely shredded lettuce heart, whole green peas and a hint of cream.

* Bouquet garni is a little package of herbs, celery and bay leaf tied in a bundle using the outside leaf of a green leek.

'

Fresh produce in South Africa has dramatically improved in variety and quality. Modern technology means that seasonal scarcity is almost a thing of the past.

,

sushi

The food that swept the western world is becoming increasingly popular in South Africa. Sushi is not just raw fish, but an exciting array of many different types of food wrapped around special Japanese rice, spiced with a dash of wasabi mustard* and served with soya sauce and finely sliced pickled ginger. I was instrumental in opening the first Japanese restaurant in South Africa at the Elangeni Sun Hotel in Durban 1984, and my love of sushi dates back to the time I spent in Japan.

Assorted fresh fish and shellfish, e.g.
  tuna (the belly is the best)
  red roman
  fresh salmon
  prawns
  calamari

Sushi rice dressing
500ml rice vinegar
60g sugar
20ml salt
2,5cm kelp

Sushi rice
340g rice
700ml water
5ml salt

wasabi mustard
seaweed for garnish

Blanch shellfish and cool.
To make the dressing, mix all the ingredients together and keep refrigerated.
Wash the raw rice well (at least 3 times in cold, running water) and drain well. Bring the water to the boil, add the rice and boil briskly for 10 minutes.
Remove from the heat and allow to stand for 5 minutes, then remove from the pan and keep covered.
Add the sushi dressing and mix together.
Shape into small barrel-shaped lozenges and top with a pinch of green wasabi mustard, then the fish or other items.
Wrap with a strip of seaweed for garnish.

Suggestion
A thin sheet of seaweed can be laid out, followed by a thin layer of cooked rice. Then add flaked crab meat, strips of crisp cucumber and spring onions. Roll up into a cone and serve.

* Wasabi mustard, made from the wasabi mustard seed, is obtainable from most oriental food outlets.

‘

As South Africa becomes more united, as the people mix and match and work together, we certainly will see the emergence of a truly South African cuisine. We at the South African Chefs Association are aware of this development, which we would like to call Rainbow Cuisine, using, as it does, all the different ingredients and influences to create a melting pot of flavours.

’

poached salmon with saffron fusion

Serves 4

4 x 70g salmon steaks, deboned and skinned
butter
4 sticks of baby celery, cut into fine slices on the angle
2 baby leeks, cut into julienne strips
freshly ground white pepper
pinch of rock salt
100ml Chardonnay wine
200ml light fish stock
5g saffron or a pinch of turmeric
50g tomato flesh, skinned, deseeded and diced
4 sprigs watercress

Take a heavy-based pot with a lid, just large enough to hold the four salmon steaks. Preheat the pan, add the butter and allow to sizzle. Add celery and leeks and cook gently for 2 minutes. Add the salmon steaks and season with pepper and rock salt. Cover with wine and fish stock, then add saffron, cover with a lid and poach gently for 6 minutes.
Remove salmon from the liquid and keep warm. Briskly reduce the stock and wine mixture by half. Add diced tomato and watercress and adjust seasoning.
To serve, place a bed of celery and leeks coated with the saffron stock in a soup bowl. Place the salmon on top.
Serve hot accompanied by a spring salad.

Suggestion
Garlic and a variety of fresh herbs can be added if you prefer a stronger flavour, but for me the salmon must be the champion.

'

Food is gentle: treat it with dignity. I learnt this from a chef I was working with when I was 14 years old. I was washing lettuce very roughly over a sink. He explained that lettuce was as delicate as a lady's breast and if one man-handled food one could not expect to get good results.

'

medallions of ostrich – pride of Oudtshoorn

Our ostrich is famed in other countries and not often featured on South African menus.

Serves 4
8 x 50g ostrich fillets
salt & ground black pepper
olive oil & butter

Grilled vegetables
16 slices of carrot
16 slices of butternut
16 slices baby marrow
8 baby sweetcorn
16 slices sweet potato
8 wedges of leek
15–30ml fresh parsely, chopped
garlic, chopped
olive oil

Mealie croquettes
200g cooked maize meal
knob of butter
salt & pepper
flour
1 egg, beaten
desiccated coconut

Marinade
1 part plain yoghurt
2 parts red wine
mixed herbs

Sauce
100ml prepared meat gravy
50ml Amarula liqueur
15ml marinade

To cook the vegetables, place them in a single layer on a baking dish (do not use any oil) and grill both sides until golden brown. Drizzle with olive oil and sprinkle with the garlic and parsley. Prepare maize meal into a thick porridge, using water, and allow to cool. Add butter and seasoning, mix and form into croquette shapes. Dip into the flour, then into the beaten egg and roll in the coconut. Deep-fry until golden brown.
To make the marinade, mix all the ingredients together and marinate ostich fillets for 6 hours. Remove steaks, dry well and season with salt and lots of black pepper. Sauté in the oil and butter until medium rare. Remove from the pan and keep warm.
To make the sauce, remove excess grease from the pan used for cooking ostrich steaks, add the liqueur, gravy and the marinade. Bring to the boil and pour around the steaks.

"

South African cuisine is a melting pot of a variety of flavours. Necessity brought about cooking methods like pickling, braaiing and the drying of food. We must take these methods forward and give them a modern feel.

Bill Gallagher

"

This enigmatic duo, both formally trained as teachers, have jointly put together eight cookbooks. The market for South African-produced cookbooks was very new and undeveloped in the early 1980s and their innovative, full-colour manuals took a market starved of locally produced cookery material by storm. Their flair for food has won them great favour in our emerging South African market – not only as cookbook authors, but also as food stylists, food writers and cookery teachers. It is their sound, no-nonsense approach to food, never-fail recipes and excellent ideas, that have made them household names.

A free spirit and desire to do things on her own saw Shirley Guy start her own cookery school, The Dough Hook, at her home in Bedfordview 21 years ago. It is a bustling enviroment, in which she educates and stimulates palates with a whole host of international food ideas from basic Italian to a taste of Asia.

Marty Klinzman, an American by birth, has made South Africa her home since early 1970. She is well known as the home economist for Kenwood Home Appliances and is a sought-after food stylist.

Marty Klinzman

Shirley Guy

man '

In the 25 plus years I've been writing, teaching and talking about food in South Africa, I've seen many changes! Lifestyles are so busy! We now want good food that doesn't take forever to prepare. I think I have helped with that – by presenting food that makes good use of time-saving appliances, by encouraging cooks to make the best of our 'convenience' foods and by introducing new flavours from other lands to liven up local produce. It has always been my aim to give ideas that people can really use. It's part of the success of my recipes. No 'coffee table' cooking – just good-looking, great-tasting food!

Marty Klinzman

, '

I love the seasons, and can picture the wonderful selection of fresh fruit, vegetables and flowers now available at the greengrocer. We can choose from the most tropical, large, fleshy mangoes, to the finest of berries – even delicate raspberries are there for the taking during the course of the year. There is a growing interest in ethnic foods. Good Italian products are everywhere, and tasty morsels from Asia suddenly fascinate those who love to eat or cook. The cross-pollination is such, that even the traditional braai lives harmoniously side-by-side with the barbeque.

Shirley Guy

,

Shirley Guy

fusion butternut soup with quick focaccia

Old fashioned flavours we know and love are livened up with a touch of the East, by adding ingredients such as lemon grass, cumin, coriander and mango.

Serves 6

30ml oil
1 onion, chopped
½ clove garlic, minced
1 stalk lemon grass, split, or substitute
    20ml prepared, sliced lemon grass
½ small chilli, seeded
1 apple, peeled and chopped
500g butternut, chopped
2ml gound cumin
30ml fresh coriander
850ml chicken stock
½ fresh mango
salt and pepper to taste
splash lemon juice
fresh coriander
yoghurt

Focaccia
15ml instant dry yeast
330g bread flour
5ml salt
pinch of sugar
10ml fresh parsley, chopped
3ml crushed rosemary
3ml each thyme and oregano
250ml lukewarm water
coarse salt
chopped garlic
fresh rosemary
a little olive oil

Heat the oil and sauté onion, garlic, lemon grass, chilli and apple for about 3 minutes. Add butternut, cumin, coriander and stock. Simmer until vegetables are tender.

Purée the soup with mango in a liquidizer or with a hand blender, then gently reheat to serve. Season to taste and add lemon juice. Garnish with fresh coriander and a swirl of yoghurt.

To make the focaccia, combine the yeast, flour, salt, sugar and herbs in the bowl of an electric mixer. Add enough of the lukewarm water so that the dough forms a ball. Knead with the mixer for about 4 minutes. Then turn dough out on a lightly floured surface. Cover and let it rest for 15 minutes.

Divide the dough into two and roll each piece into a circle. Make a few slashes across the dough, or make indentations with your knuckles. Sprinkle with coarse salt, chopped garlic and rosemary. Drizzle a little olive oil over and bake at 200°C for 15–20 minutes. Serve warm.

'

Today the aim in cooking is to taste real food. Food is no longer masked with those sprinkle-spread things we could buy in the seventies.

Marty Klinzman

,

spiced grilled chicken with grilled vegetables

The spiced chicken and grilled vegetables have a distinct Californian flavour! Make up the spice and have it on hand to use with fish, steak and even hamburgers. I cook this quick, healthy dish on a table top grill.

Serves 6

6-8 skinless, boneless chicken breasts

Spice mixture
8ml coarse salt
10ml mixed peppercorns, or black peppercorns
15ml finely grated orange rind, dried
10ml cumin seeds
3ml ground ginger
5ml dried parsley
3ml dried thyme
1/2 cinnamon stick
3ml sugar
8ml coriander seeds
5ml chilli powder
1 whole clove

Vegetables
2 red or green peppers
2 baby marrows, cut in strips lengthwise
1 medium brinjal, sliced lengthwise
1 red onion, sliced into rings
a little olive oil
salt & pepper
fresh rosemary and sage leaves

Combine all the ingredients for the spice mixture in a spice mill and blend until finely ground or grind with a mortar and pestle. Sprinkle a light coating over both sides of the chicken breast and place chicken on a hot table top grill, or grill in the oven or on the braai. Chicken breasts are quick to cook, so grill each side for only about 4 minutes. Serve hot with the vegetables and jasmine rice or serve cold with salad.
To make the vegetables, cut peppers lengthwise into wide strips and remove the seeds. Brush all vegetables with olive oil and lay them on a table top grill (under a hot grill in the oven, or on the braai). (Lay some sprigs of rosemary and sage on the grill to give extra flavour.) Grill until nicely browned, then sprinkle with salt and pepper and turn vegetables to grill on the other side.
Serve warm with the chicken, or store grilled vegetables in olive oil with rosemary and garlic to serve with salads.

'

It's a worldwide trend: busy people demand food that looks and tastes good with the minimum of effort. They are buying the freshest ingredients and semi-convenient items that they can make into a meal quickly.
Marty Klinzman

,

fresh fruit with cream & brulée topping

Serves 6

750ml seasonal fruit such as strawberries or
    raspberries, sliced nectarines or peaches, sliced
    bananas or even gooseberries
30ml brandy or cream sherry
a little granulated sugar
190ml cream
125ml mascarpone cheese
125ml castor sugar
50ml water

Garnish
fresh fruit
mint

Slice your favourite combination of fruit and place in an ovenproof dish. Sprinkle with brandy or sherry and a little granulated sugar. Whip the cream to stiff peaks, fold in the mascarpone and spread over the fruit. The dish can now be refrigerated for an hour or so.

To serve, place castor sugar and water into a small saucepan over very low heat to make the caramel. Stir to dissolve the sugar completely. Then increase heat and bring the mixture to the boil. Do not stir the mixture, just cook until syrup turns a rich caramel colour.

Remove the fruit mixture from the refrigerator and drizzle the caramel over the cream in a decorative pattern with a spoon or fork. The caramel will set immediately.

Serve within about 30 minutes, garnished with fresh fruit and mint if desired.

Note: The caramel can be made in the microwave oven. Place water and sugar in a heavy jug or bowl. Microwave on full power for 1 minute, checking the colour. Then microwave on 50% power for 3 minutes or so, checking the colour until it is rich golden brown.

People in South Africa are looking for lighter, quicker and better quality food tastes. In a hectic lifestyle this can only be achieved with indispensible kitchen appliances. Items like microwave ovens are an absolute necessity and food processors are merely extensions of the working hand.

Marty Klinzman

'

*Now that one can get almost all the Asian ingredients including the conve-
nience foods in South Africa, there is a growing interest in Oriental cooking.*

Shirley Guy

,

steamed langoustine salad with dipping sauces

Serves 8

16–24 langoustines, cleaned
a few pieces of lemon grass
a few slices of fresh ginger
mixed salad leaves
1–2 mangoes, peeled and sliced

Thai style chilli sauce
200g sugar
200ml white vinegar
3 garlic cloves, crushed
5ml ginger juice (grate a piece of fresh ginger and
    squeeze out juice)
2 red chillies
10ml mild chilli sauce

Tofu dip
1 garlic clove, crushed
10 ml lemon juice
25ml light soya sauce
1 block tofu, drained
30ml fresh coriander, chopped
25–50ml Italian olive oil

Place langoustines in a bamboo steamer, add
the lemon grass and ginger and steam for 5–8
minutes, depending on size.
Remove langoustines from the shells and,
allowing 2–3 per person, serve with the salad
leaves, sliced mango and dipping sauces.
To make the chilli sauce, boil all the sauce
ingredients until slightly syrupy, about 10 minutes. Allow to cool before serving.
To make the tofu dip, blend all the ingredients
up to and including the coriander, in a liquidiser
or food processor until smooth. Add sufficient
oil to thicken the sauce.

'

Some would say that Karoo lamb, raised on a sparse diet of fragrant herbs, is the most succulent and tasty in the world.

Shirley Guy

,

lamb with green peppercorn marinade

Serves 8

1 butterflied leg of lamb, 1,25kg (reserve the bones)

Marinade
45ml green peppercorns
15ml fresh rosemary
60ml fresh mint, chopped
1-2 garlic cloves, crushed
60ml lemon juice
60ml light soya sauce

Topping
30ml Dijon mustard
3ml coarse salt

Sauce
lamb bones
1 litre water
250ml red wine
1 stick celery, chopped
1 carrot, chopped
1 onion, chopped
1 bay leaf
parsley sprigs
30ml redcurrant or quince jelly
50ml red muscadel
10ml cake flour
10ml butter

Combine the marinade ingredients and pour them over the lamb. Refrigerate for 12–24 hours, turning the meat from time to time. Drain and pat dry, reserving the marinade.
Spread mustard over meat, sprinkle with salt and roast at 220°C for 40 minutes or until meat is just pink.
To make the sauce, place bones, water, wine, vegetables and seasonings in a large saucepan. Cover and bring to the boil. Simmer for 1 hour, then remove the cover and boil rapidly to reduce to about 350ml. Strain and add about half the marinade then boil for a further 5 minutes. Add redcurrant jelly and muscadel. Combine the butter and flour, add to the sauce and stir until thickened.
Carve meat and serve with the sauce.

panna cotta with catawba sauce

Catawba is a small, dark grape variety, common in Gauteng gardens, with a tough outer skin and fragrant scent.

Serves 8

Cream
1 litre of cream
150ml castor sugar
5ml vanilla essence
90ml milk
30ml water
25 ml gelatine

Catawba sauce
750g catawbas* (other grapes can be used)
350ml water
about 50ml sugar
300ml red wine
15ml cornflour
a little water to combine

Heat the cream and sugar and simmer for 10 minutes. Remove from heat and add vanilla. Combine the milk, water and gelatine and stand for 5 minutes. Heat, either over boiling water or in a microwave at 50% for 60 seconds, until gelatine has dissolved.

Add to the cream, pour into 8–10 moulds lightly sprayed with non-stick cooking spray and refrigerate for 3–4 hours.

To serve, dip into hot water, 'introduce' a little air by gently loosening the edges with a sharp knife and turn onto plates. Pour sauce over a portion of each mould and a little around the edges. Garnish with a few grapes.

To make the sauce, rinse the grapes and place them in a pan, crushing them slightly. Add the water and sugar, bring to the boil and simmer for 15 minutes. Cool and strain.

Boil the red wine separately until it has reduced by half. Add to the strained juice. Combine cornflour with a little water and add to the sauce, stirring over a low heat until thickened.

Alternative
1 packet of summer berries can be used instead of the grapes.

'

Long-term freezing of food is a thing of the past. If you make anything for your freezer and have not used it in three weeks, then you will never need it. The quality of fresh ingredients has become really good in recent times.

Shirley Guy

'

Lucas Ndlo

'

My friends in the area surrounding the Coach House supply
all our ingredients – everything's grown around our hotel! So
it just comes naturally to provide the choicest South African
dishes. There is a Bonsmara cattle farm in the area which
produces the finest beef, fresh trout from the Drakensberg,
our own farm produces vegetables, avocados, mangoes and
nuts and all the farmers around Tzaneen let us know when
they have something special – fresh horseradish, green
peppercorns, and much more.

'

Born in Pretoria, the son of a Zionist priest, Lucas Ndlovu started work in the kitchen of the Santa Barbara Hotel. It was here, under the guidance of a Swiss chef, that his culinary skills developed. In 1980, having worked at a number of different hotels, including the famed President Hotel in Johannesburg, a serious car accident brought his career to a halt for almost three years. A chance meeting with Guy Matthews, in 1983, led to an offer of employment, as Executive Chef at the new Coach House Country Hotel in Agatha, in the north-eastern Transvaal. This historical site was originally one of the 'outspans' for the Abbot Downing mail coaches, which were often in danger from a local highwayman who preyed on travellers. With Ndlovu as the head chef, the hotel serves wonderful unpretentious food using some of the finest ingredients found in abundance in the area.

As a member of The South African Chefs Association, Lucas has represented South Africa on many occasions at various events. In 1989 he was the first black African team member and his first course entry of crayfish and crocodile took first prize in the *Bocuse d'Or* competition in the same year.

On a recent promotional tour to Norway, Ndlovu was the flavour of the month. The traditional South African favourites he served – like bobotie and yellow rice and venison, followed by pecan nut pie and koeksisters – were extremely popular with the locals.

'

Avocado is at its very best when eaten fresh. I have experimented with cooking it in a number of ways and have failed.

,

avocado mmamathola

I developed this recipe using the wonderful combination of beef-flavoured consommé with the creamy, smooth texture of the avocado.

Serves 6

3 ripe Fuerte or Hass avocados
lemon juice
350ml home-made beef consommé, well chilled
100ml sour cream, thickened
45ml chives, snipped
1 small jar lumpfish roe

Carefully halve avocados and remove the pips.
Remove the skin without damaging the flesh.
Brush cut edges and hollows with lemon juice.
Fill cavities with spoonfuls of jellied consommé.
Top each with a spoonful of sour cream.
Sprinkle chives on the cream and top with caviar.
Serve on a bed of fresh green salad.

Note: A good consommé starts with a good rich stock, in this case made with beef, clear of fat, then made crystal clear by clarification. Beaten egg whites and their shells are added to the simmering stock. As the egg whites cook, they attract and hold the tiny particles of fat and other matter that cloud the soup. When this mass of solids has been strained through a sieve, the liquid that comes through is a sparkling, clear consommé. If soup is not jellied enough, sponge 2,5ml gelatine in 10ml water, melt and add to hot soup. When cool, refrigerate until jellied and use as above.

smoked trout kedgeree

The wonderful fresh trout found in the Northern Province can be prepared in many different ways, fresh or smoked. A favourite way of mine is to replace haddock with smoked trout in this popular breakfast dish. The mixture should be slightly wet and is delicious served on toast.

Serves 4

150g cooked rice
100g butter
450g smoked trout, skinned and flaked
1 small onion, finely chopped
7ml curry powder or to taste
5ml tomato purée
65ml fish stock or water
2 eggs boiled for 8 minutes and cooled quickly in cold
    water
150ml cream
2 raw eggs

Garnish
Lemon slices
parsley, chopped

Preheat oven to 180°C. Place rice in a dish and cover with foil. Place in the oven and heat for 15 minutes.
Melt 50g of butter in a frying pan and toss fish in the pan until warm. Mix fish together with rice. Sauté onion in remaining butter until soft. Add curry powder. Cook for a minute.
Add tomato purée and stock or water and cook for 2 minutes, stirring frequently, then cool. Add roughly chopped hardboiled eggs to rice and fish and combine well with a fork.
Beat cream and raw egg together, add to the cooled curry sauce and stir. Combine this with the rice mixture in an ovenproof dish.
Return to oven for 5 minutes and allow to warm thoroughly.
Serve garnished with lemon and parsley.

'

I don't smoke, I don't go to parties, I don't drink, but I just love eating good food.

,

pan-fried Sabie trout stuffed with spinach and served with pecan nut butter

Serves 4

4 medium sized trout, approx. 250g each, deboned
*   from stomach side*
500g spinach leaves, coarsely chopped
60g butter
salt and pepper
150g butter
lemon juice

Pecan butter
200g butter
40ml lemon juice
salt and pepper
25ml pecan nuts, chopped
20ml pecan nuts, chopped for garnish

Clean and dry the trout with a paper towel. Wash spinach and wipe dry. Melt the butter in a saucepan over a moderate heat and cook the spinach until it is tender. Remove from heat and squeeze to remove liquid.

Season trout inside and out. Place remaining 150g butter in a heavy frying pan over a moderate heat. Allow butter to begin sizzling. Splay trout open side down into sizzling butter. Allow to brown slightly. Turn the trout over and place 1 quarter of spinach lengthways inside each fish. Close the fish and allow to cook for 2–4 minutes on either side, at a moderate heat. Sprinkle with lemon juice.

To make the pecan butter, cream the butter, lemon juice, salt, pepper and pecans until soft. Roll butter into 2,5cm diameter roll and chill. Cut into slices as required.

Place slices of butter onto each fish and top with chopped pecans. Serve at once.

macadamia pie with banana ice cream and fudge sauce

In Tzaneen we have plenty of tropical ingredients to work with. Bananas make a delicious dessert and nuts the perfect accompaniment.

Serves 8–10

Pastry
200g cake flour
pinch of salt
125g butter
1 egg yolk
15ml cooking oil
about 60ml iced water

Filling
250g castor sugar
125ml cake flour
125ml maple syrup
200g crushed macadamia nuts
3 eggs
pinch of salt
75g butter

Topping
30ml butter, melted
50g roasted macadamia nuts
60ml icing sugar

Banana ice cream
4–5 ripe bananas
juice of half a lemon
100g castor sugar
15ml white rum
300ml cream, whipped

To make the pastry, rub the cake flour, salt and butter together. Add yolk, cooking oil and enough ice water until it just binds. Roll out and line a pie plate.

For the filling, mix all the ingredients together in a large bowl, except for the butter. Melt the butter and add to the mixture. Mix thoroughly. Pour the mixture into the uncooked crust. Bake at 180°C for 40–45 minutes. Leave to cool and brush the filling with 30ml of hot melted butter.

For the topping, crush roasted macadamia nuts and sprinkle over the pie while the butter is still hot. Sieve icing sugar over the pie and place under the grill until the sugar caramelises.

For the ice cream, blend the bananas, lemon juice, rum and sugar until smooth. Fold in the whipped cream. Place in a container with a tight-fitting lid and freeze until firm.

Serve with macadamia pie.

'

A man who can cook can command much respect in a community.

Lucas Ndlovu

'

Lyndall Pop

'

I was accustomed from a very early age to eating exotic food. My grandmother was a great entertainer and I grew up savouring the buzz around food. I often think back to the 1950s in South Africa – opulent times of great entertainment and the most marvellous parties. This was huge and wonderful, traditional South African hospitality. Food then had a very traditional English style to it. My great influence in food has been the cookery writer Elizabeth David. Her ideas on food are good and sound. Remember, this was just after the war when the good, honest treatment of food was what was desired. Her food philosophy was so refreshing and introduced many marvellous fresh flavours into cookery.

,

Lyndall Popper

er

Despite a dream of making a career on the stage, Lyndall Popper was steered into a more academic qualification – her father felt that nice girls did not study at the Royal Academy of Dramatic Arts! This led her first into a legal stint at Rhodes University, followed by the completion of a BA at Wits University with English as a major.

It was both economics and her love of cooking that turned Lyndall into a caterer of note. This occupation allowed her flexibility while bringing up her family of five.

She has built a large following after a 15 year sojourn as food editor of *The Star's* Angela Day column, which brought her right into the homes and hearts of thousands of newspaper readers. She is well known for her great knowledge and writing on the subject, her sound and unfussy food philosophy and innovative recipes.

Lyndall has made the theatre of food her career. Author of two books, *Herbs for the Table* and *Fine Foods on the Highveld,* she is presently the senior food editor of *Food and Home* magazine and is based in Johannesburg.

There is a new generation of fast-food gourmets. Soup — my very favourite food — falls into the fast-food category. New eating styles show that soup is no longer just part of a meal — it is the meal. Boontjiesop, an old South African recipe, can be brought into the forefront of modern cuisine.

bean soup with chilli-touched sundried tomatoes

This traditional soup becomes a complete meal when you sharpen its marvellous earthy taste with a zap of lemon, top it with crumbled feta cheese, a hint of chilli and lemon rind, then accompany it with a robust slice of homemade olive bread.

Serves 6 – 8

250g haricot beans, soaked overnight in water
*   to cover*
250–300g (4–6) lamb riblets
1 large onion, stuck with a whole clove
1 parsnip
1 turnip
1 bay leaf
a few sprigs each celery and parsley
salt
freshly ground black pepper
8 sundried tomatoes in oil, drained and sliced
3 red chillies, finely sliced

Drain the beans and place them in a deep, heavy-based saucepan. Add the following ingredients up to and including the celery and parsley. Cover with 2 litres of cold tap water, bring to the boil, skimming off any scum that rises to the surface. Adjust the heat to simmer and cook uncovered until the beans are tender – perhaps 2 hours.

Remove the riblets and cut the meat from the bones, reserving it in bite-sized pieces. Remove and discard the flavouring vegetables.

Season to taste and simmer another 5 minutes. Return the reserved lamb pieces to the soup with the sundried tomato slivers and the chopped chillies. Heat through and serve.

Note: For absolute fatless perfection, cool and chill the soup after returning the lamb pieces to it. This way any fat will collect and congeal on the surface and may be easily skimmed off.

'

The nineties have seen the start of a movement away from heavier dishes to a demand for food that can be cooked more quickly or even eaten raw. As a result, I see an increase in the use of zesty flavourings like lemon, herbs, sun-dried tomatoes, olives and the like.

,

avocado and orange salad on spinach with smoked salmon trout

The fast-food trend also accounts for the popularity and mingling of Eastern flavours into our cuisine. This salad – inspired by a recipe in *Old Food* by Jill Dupleix – expresses all these sentiments.

Serves 2 as a lunch dish or 4 as a first course

300g baby spinach leaves or equivalent normal spinach
2 medium avocado pears
2 oranges, cut into segments
200g smoked trout, cut in wide strips
a few chives for garnish

Dressing
60ml fresh orange juice
rind of ¹/₂ orange, finely grated
1 clove garlic, chopped
3ml salt
3ml white pepper
60ml olive oil
5ml cumin seeds, placed in a small saucepan over a moderate heat until they start toasting and are fragrant

Make the dressing first. Place the orange juice and rind into a cup and add the garlic, salt and pepper, whisking with a fork until the salt dissolves. Whisk in the olive oil oil until the mixture thickens. Stir in toasted cumin seeds.
Pour ³/₄ of the dressing over the spinach and toss to coat the leaves. Place on a serving plate.
Peel the avocado pears and cut across into crescents. Pile these over the spinach with the orange segments and smoked trout strips.
Drizzle with the remaining dressing, garnish with the chives and serve at once with crusty bread.

'

The great interest in polenta and all things Italian has brought this staple of the Mediterranean into the forefront of food talk. In South Africa we have mealie meal — the fragrant, white kind beloved by many local people.

'

mealie meal with two sauces

Serves 4

Mealie meal
750ml boiling water
5ml salt
375ml mealie meal
250ml mealie kernels, cut from freshly cooked cobs, or
   use canned sweetcorn kernels
30ml olive oil

Mushroom sauce
25g dried mushrooms
1 large onion, finely chopped
30ml olive oil
4 large brown mushrooms, sliced
45ml dry sherry
15–45ml cream

Chillied fresh tomato sauce
1 large onion, finely sliced
3 chillies, finely sliced
30ml olive oil
1 clove garlic, crushed with 5ml salt
1 x 420g can Italian whole, peeled tomatoes with juice
4 medium, ripe tomatoes, peeled, seeded and cut into
   crescents
salt
freshly ground black pepper
a little sugar to taste (optional)

To cook the mealie meal, boil the water in a saucepan, add the salt and stir in the mealie meal. Cover and cook over a low heat for 5 minutes, stirring frequently to prevent the mixture catching and burning.
Add mealie kernels, cover and continue cooking in the same way for another 10 minutes. Remove from the heat, stir in olive oil and add additional seasoning. Using a fluted cutter, cut the mixture into rounds, brush with olive oil and grill.
To make the mushroom sauce, soak dried mushrooms in water for at least 30 minutes and then chop finely. Reserve the soaking liquid.
Combine the onion and oil in a saucepan and cook gently for 5 minutes without allowing the onion to burn. Increase heat, add the brown mushrooms and cook them over a high heat, stirring until they are almost cooked through.
Add the sherry and boil fast for 30 seconds to disperse the alcohol. Add 60ml of the soaking water and simmer a minute. Finally stir in a little cream and season to taste.
To make the chilli tomato sauce, combine onion and chillies with the olive oil and cook covered over a low heat for 5 minutes, stirring now and again. Add the garlic and salt mixture and cook for another minute uncovered. Increase the heat and add the canned tomatoes and juice, crushing them a little with a spoon. Cook uncovered over a moderate heat for 10 minutes, stirring now and again. Cook until mixture has reduced by half. Add the tomato crescents and season to taste. Cook uncovered until the tomato crescents are cooked through, but not overdone.
Serve mealie meal rounds with the two sauces.

'

Producers and manufacturers are now making it possible for all of us to come together around tables on which we serve quickly prepared, fresh and inviting 'fusion style' dishes drawing on all the delicious traditions of our diverse heritage.

,

mussels with a touch of Thai

This variation of an old dish made famous by French fishermen brings oriental flavours into the mix, using excellent South African mussels and fruity white wine to great effect.

Serves 4

750ml or 1 bottle fruity white wine
30ml fresh ginger, grated
2 cloves garlic, crushed with 5 ml salt
25g fresh coriander
2kg fresh mussels
salt & pepper to taste
400ml coconut milk or coconut cream

Combine the wine with the ginger, garlic and coriander in a wide-bottomed saucepan. The wine should fill the pan to a depth of 3cm. Add the mussels. Cover the saucepan, bring to the boil and boil fast for abut 3 minutes. Check progress from time to time and remove any mussels that have opened. Keep these warm until all have opened (remember that those that do not open should be discarded).

Strain the sauce, discarding the flavouring ingredients. Return the sauce to the pan, stir in coconut milk or coconut cream and season to taste then heat through.

Pour over the mussels and garnish with additional coriander sprigs. Serve with French bread.

'

*During my stint as a caterer, I discovered that
I spent every weekend in someone else's
kitchen and never my own. Home cooking is
the best because it is cooked with love.*

Lyndall Popper

'

Garth Shu

Garth Shnier, executive chef of The Michelangelo Hotel on Sandton Square (renowned for its very own style of cuisine), has created and designed food which represents a combination of traditional Africa, infusing Cape Malay, Madagascan and tribal styles.

A South African by birth, Shnier feels he has his grandmother to thank for laying the foundations for a career in food. He has fond memories of her marvellous home cooking – bread, rice puddings and rusks – all prepared on a large coal stove. His food career has spanned many years and has seen him working in various hotels and restaurants countrywide, including a stint at a top class international restaurant in Germany.

Possessing, by his own admission, a very competitive streak, Shnier has made a rapid rise on the South African culinary scene. He feels he owes much to his mentor, Garth Stroebel (Executive Group Chef of Orient Express Hotels) and the South African Chefs Association for his advancement in the food industry.

Garth Shnier

'

I received my training in some of the finest kitchens of South Africa. As a chef you must always acknowledge your debts to others: men like Bill Gallagher, Garth Stroebel and Heinz Imhoff – pioneers in visionary cooking in South Africa – had a tremendous influence on me. Today, I continue to draw inspiration from dining at the fine establishments of all my contemporaries but have also looked to the source of my cooking – the great regional cuisine of Germany – for some basic grounding.

While classical cooking has been my foundation and my inspiration, my culinary style has changed tremendously through the years. When I think of *beurre blanc* I made ten years ago, I know I couldn't eat it today. It was a wonderfully lavish reduction of large amounts of butter and cream, but of course like my customers I want to be thin not fat! Customers want the wonderful flavours but they are very conscious of lightness – not only in flavour but also in style. That has been one of my greatest yet most inspiring challenges! To achieve the goal our customers set for us, we need better combinations of ingredients and techniques – cooking needs to evolve to stay fresh. We even beat air into our sauces these days, to make them lighter!

One of the main objectives of cooking is to maintain and highlight the intrinsic flavour. Why make it more complicated? Freshness is number one ... The simpler the food, the more important the ingredients. In a great dish, you can see, eat, taste and smell everything. No one thing is overpowering. These days, my obsession is to extract as much flavour as possible to make a sauce that is as light as possible. When I cook, I don't like to confuse the palate with too much going on. My goal is to perfectly balance three different flavours in a dish. If I achieve this, I know I have created an apotheosis, a quintessence, of all three flavours – a dish that is much more than the sum of its parts.

,

crown of asparagus with spiced couscous

Set on avocado with papino salsa, dressed with slivers of hot, paperbark-smoked ostrich and infused with a red pepper marmalade.

Serves 4

20g ostrich fillet
100g paperbark and bluegum shavings*
2 punnets green asparagus
1 leek, cooked
6 rocket leaves
4 lolla rossa (heart leaves)

Papino salsa
2 avocados, stoned and peeled
1 papino, peeled and seeded
60ml fresh coriander
1–2 chillies (according to taste)
1 spring onion, chopped

Red pepper marmalade
2 red peppers
1 onion
3 garlic cloves
60ml red wine vinegar
30ml brown sugar
15ml olive oil
salt and freshly ground pepper
60g spiced couscous salad
5ml olive oil
1 clove garlic, crushed
1 red pepper, finely chopped
6 button mushroons finely chopped
fresh ground pepper

Garnish
red, green and yellow peppers, finely chopped
baked sweet potato, sliced
8 French chives

Seal off ostrich and place in smoker with paperbark and bluegum shavings.* Smoke until pink and succulent then leave to rest in a warm place.

Prepare a salsa from the avocado, papino, coriander, chillies and spring onion.

Bring a pan of salted water to the boil. Add asparagus and cook for 3–4 minutes. Remove asparagus when tender, but still crisp. Place in iced water to stop further cooking.

Cut off stalk ends from asparagus leaving a 7cm tip. Cut spears in half lengthwise. Meanwhile chop off-cuts finely and add to salsa.

Carefully surround salsa mound with halved asparagus spears, making sure the tips hang over the top, giving a crown effect.

Cut four thin strips from the cooked leek and tie around prepared mould. Place salad in centre of crown. Surround asparagus with lettuce, remaining juices and pepper marmalade then garnish as illustrated.

To make marmalade, halve, core and deseed red peppers. Chop peppers, onion and garlic roughly. Place in a small heavy-based pan together with remaining ingredients and simmer for about 1 hour. Stir from time to time, until nearly all the liquid has evaporated and the mixtue is dense and shiny. Serve at room temperature.

* Bluegum and paperbark shavings are available from speciality outdoor stores.

'

I think 'infusion food' better describes modern cuisine than the often bandied 'fusion food' label. Our emerging South African cuisine is progressive African 'infusion food.'

,

Norwegian salmon, lightly scented with bluegum woodshavings & lemon

Accompanied by a crisp potato fan and vegetables placed on a sparkling wine cream sauce.

Serves 4

2 large potatoes, scrubbed and thinly sliced
1 punnet baby corn
1 punnet baby carrots
2 okra
4 sheets spring roll pastry
1 root celeriac bulb
half a fresh Norwegian salmon fillet with skin on
salt & pepper
olive oil
100g lemon leaves
100g bluegum shavings*
4 medium pieces oak tree bark

Sauce
200ml fish velouté
100ml pouring cream
50g fennel leaves, chopped
50g French chives, chopped
100ml sparkling wine

Garnish
herb bouquet, per plate

Brush potatoes with olive oil and bake in a slow oven. Keep warm. Cut baby corn, baby carrots and okra in batons and blanch.
Shape spring roll pastry into horns and bake. Fill with blanched vegetables once the horn has cooled. Clean celeriac root, leaving stems on, and cut into wedges, blanch and grill-mark.
Cut fish into portions, and season. Seal off with olive oil in a hot saucepan.
Prepare smoker with bluegum shavings. Place lemon leaves on oak tree bark and top with fish. Smoke until pink and succulent.
Bring fish velouté to a simmer. Add cream, chopped fennel, chives and leave to infuse. Strain through a fine muslin cloth.
Whisk sauce, add sparkling wine and use immediately.
Place sauce on a warm dinner plate. Leaving fish on leaves, remove from smoker and position on the plate. Arrange vegetable filled horn and celeriac on plate. Wedge potato between fish and bark.
Garnish with herb bouquet garni and serve.

* Bluegum shavings are available from speciality outdoor stores.

Cajun spiced chicken breast & crayfish tail

Presented on dirty rice, tempura vegetables laced with wasabi and mango dressing.

Serves 4

4 chicken breasts
Cajun spices
4 crayfish tails
salt
lemon pepper

Dirty rice
200g wild rice
butter and oil
150g chicken livers
1 garlic clove, finely chopped
1 onion, finely chopped
6 mushrooms, finely chopped
300ml water

Tempura vegetables
oil for frying
extra flour for coating
175ml iced water
30g plain flour
1 egg
5ml chopped parsley
1 head of broccoli florets
8 baby sweetcorn
2 carrots cut into batons
4 courgettes cut into batons

Wasabi*
15ml wasabi
30ml chicken stock
45ml cream

Mango dressing
2 ripe mangoes, peeled
20ml olive oil
10ml white wine vinegar
salt & pepper

poppadoms, for garnish

Coat chicken breasts in prepared Cajun spices. Cut crayfish tails in half lengthwise and season with salt and lemon pepper.

Bring salted water to the boil. Add rice and cook for 10 minutes or until cooked through.

Heat butter and a little oil in a frying pan (this stops the butter from burning). Add chicken livers. Once they are cooked, chop roughly. Add garlic and rest of ingredients to the pan, making sure it does not burn. Fry for 2–3 minutes. Combine with chicken livers and rice and set aside.

To make the tempura batter, whisk all the ingredients, up to parsley, together. Coat the prepared vegetables in flour. Heat oil in a deep fryer.

Dip the vegetables into the batter and deep-fry until crisp and golden.

In a pan, shallow fry the chicken breasts until cooked through. Grill crayfish tails with a little butter (1–2 minutes on each side).

To make the wasabi, combine the ingredients together.

To make mango dressing, remove pips and combine olive oil, vinegar and seasoning, then pass through a fine strainer.

To serve, place breasts and crayfish tails on rice and surround with the wasabi and mango dressing. Garnish with deep-fried poppadoms.

* Wasabi is available from Chinese supermarkets.

loin of Karoo lamb on braised spinach

With ratatouille and crisp fried polenta accompanied by a tomato lamb jus.

Serves 4

800g lean lamb loin
250g cleaned spinach, free of stalks
2 onions, diced
50g butter
salt & pepper
1 garlic clove, peeled and chopped

Ratatouille
50g butter
2 onions, chopped
1 aubergine, chopped
2 baby marrows, chopped
1 red pepper, diced
1 green pepper, diced
2 medium tomatoes, peeled and chopped
2,5ml dried oreganum
2,5ml dried basil
1 bay leaf
1 garlic clove
salt & pepper

250g polenta or mealie meal
40g parmesan cheese, grated
50ml oil
200g butter
ground black pepper
ground nutmeg

Sauce
15 ml tomato paste
300 ml red wine
400 ml water

Cut sinews off lamb loin and keep separate. Wash spinach under running water. Blanch onions and spinach in boiling water, remove and refresh under cold water. Brown onion in butter, add spinach and salt and pepper to taste. Add garlic. Set aside and keep warm.

To make the ratatouille, heat butter and sauté onion for 3–4 minutes. Add vegetables up to and including the green pepper, and cook for 2 minutes, sauté then add the tomatoes. Add oreganum, basil and bay leaf. Stir constantly for 5 minutes, then add garlic and season to taste.

Make the polenta according to the package instructions, then mix in parmesan. Spread 1cm thick on an oiled tray. Chill in the refrigerator. Cut into four with 6–8cm round cutter.

Heat 100g butter and fry polenta discs on a low heat for 5–8 minutes until golden brown on both sides. Season with cracked pepper and nutmeg.

To prepare lamb, heat 15ml oil, season lamb with salt and pepper. Fry on all sides until required cooking stage. Set aside on a cutting board and cut the meat at a 30 degree angle, in 1cm thick slices. Set ring on a plate. Divide spinach into four portions, press into a ring and set.

To prepare the sauce, use the pot in which the meat was fried. Add sinews and fry for 5–10 minutes over a medium heat. Add some leftover pieces of onion cut-offs, tomato paste, then deglaze pan with red wine. Keep on medium heat until red wine has almost evaporated. Add water. Cover with lid and cook for 10 minutes then strain.

Divide the ratatouille into four, set on top of the spinach and press tightly. Place a polenta disc onto ratatouille and lay one by one, slightly overlapping the meat around in a circle. Serve hot with sauce.

A chef who knows how to braise food correctly knows how to cook. Once you understand the method of braising you will understand the importance of flavour.

Garth Shnier

Evonne Short is employed by the Conservation Corporation Africa as their Group Hospitality and Service manager. Together with assistant Ashley Harris, she works in the kitchens of 22 lodges all over the continent, training the staff to utilise local resources to the very best advantage.

With her innovative expertise, passion and pure zest for life, she trains chefs to uplift themselves into being much more than just cooks. Encouraged to emerge from their hot, steamy kitchens and interact with their guests on a personal level, they learn to become proud spokespeople for the food they have specially prepared.

A job at Londolozi Game Lodge, with husband Peter, laid the foundations for her African food experience. With no formal training in food, but years of excellent experience in a variety of food situations, Evonne travels the world sharing her African food experiences. In her inimitable style, she combines her food expertise with that of various lodge chefs in demonstrations of their specialities at food festivals and travel shows.

Evonne Short

'

I have eaten my way through Africa and been struck by the strong food cultures in many countries. Many of our lodge kitchens utilise traditional cooking sources – fires, termite-mound ovens and even baking in donkey boilers (fires made to heat water). We develop these local resources and work together with the kitchen team to perfect their cooking. Locally found ingredients are served and enhanced in the best possible way to make for a complete bush experience. For instance, the honey found in Zanzibar is exceptionally fragrant because of the pollen from the banana plant. By using the honey in many of the dishes, both sweet and savoury, a flavour like no other runs through the food.

Africa is filled with exciting food. The coastline produces a rich harvest of rock lobsters, abalone, prawns, red roman, yellowtail, musselcrackers and kabeljou, along with snoek and angelfish. A braai on the beach – cooking fresh kelp stuffed with crayfish, black mussels, abalone and wild parsley, a touch of Sauvignon Blanc and butter, then slowly roasted over the coals – would be hard to beat.

Then there are soups made from roasted butternut and served with chilli butter; beetroot and mampoer; green mealie bread soup with hot sweetcorn bread; racks of venison served with naartjie and chilli marmalade; milk tart in a crisp pastry flavoured with cinnamon served with green figs in a ginger syrup. We have at our disposal a wealth of tradition, unusual and mysterious wild herbs, plants and recipes. A new culture is emerging: home-made sausages, e.g. warthog and plum; wildebeest and juniper; impala and apricot; kudu, bacon and chilli. Shelves groan with jars of marula nuts; roasted African underground nuts (jungo beans); wild sage honey; pickled watermelon rind; beetroot chips; banana jam; moskonfyt; chilli jam; African ginger beer; preserved fruits in spicy syrups; macadamia oil ... there's no end to the variety.

,

We have embarked on a great journey of discovery, using traditional ingredients to create a whole new South African cuisine.

chilli crisps with yellow pepper pesto

Serves 6–8

Chilli wonton wrappers
wonton wrappers* – as many as you need
oil for frying
chilli powder
za'tar**
poppy seeds
sea salt

Yellow pepper pesto
6 yellow peppers, halved and seeded
olive oil
5 cloves of garlic
150g macadamia nuts, chopped and roasted
100ml olive oil
a handful of coriander, chopped
salt and pepper

Cut each wrapper into 3 triangles. Deep fry in hot vegetable oil until crisp and golden, then drain. Sprinkle a third of them with chilli powder, a third with za'tar and a third with poppy seeds and sea salt, to taste.
To make yellow pepper pesto, roast halved peppers with a little olive oil until soft. Place in a plastic bag and cool. Peel off skins. Place them with all the other ingredients in a blender and process until smooth. Add seasoning to taste. Serve as a dip with deep-fried seasoned wrappers.

* Available from speciality Oriental stores.
**Za'tar is a flavouring spice, consisting of a blend of powdered herbs, including marjoram, sumak and thyme. Thyme may be substituted.

Our first aim is to use ingredients from the area. Take the banana flower for example: when boiled, it can be served just like an artichoke. It is equally delicious yet so local.

grilled goat cheese in banana leaves

Serves 4

2 banana leaves
200g goat cheese
lemon pepper
dried origanum
olive oil

Wash leaves in hot water. Divide the cheese into two round shapes and place each one on a banana leaf. Season with the pepper and origanum and drizzle with olive oil.
Carefully fold the leaf over and wrap tightly. Tie closed with raffia. Grill the packages over a medium grill until the leaves are slightly charred. Open leaf to expose delectable soft cheese. Eat with grilled fruit, such as quince. The banana leaves are edible but eating them is not encouraged as they are very tough.

Part of the bush experience is witnessing the food being prepared. I always encourage guests to share in the cooking, especially when making something like a potjie. The cooking time is measured by the amount of wine that is consumed!

lamb racks with coconut, beetroot harissa & mint

Serves 6

dried African underground nuts*, soaked overnight
leeks, chopped
olive oil
samp (dried maize kernels) cooked
15ml olive oil
2 clove garlic, crushed
1 large onion, finely chopped
10ml ground cumin
5ml ground coriander
45ml beetroot harissa
30ml mint, chopped
250ml shredded coconut
2 eggs
6 racks of lamb, trimmed

Beetroot harissa
4 dried red chillies
15ml paprika
2 garlic cloves, minced
2ml coriander seeds
5ml caraway seeds
2,5ml cumin seeds
2,5ml salt
185ml beetroot, cooked and puréed
10–15ml lemon juice
olive oil

To make underground nut mixture, roast nuts and parboil. Sauté leeks in olive oil and mix with samp and nuts.

Heat oil in frying pan, add garlic and onion and cook over low heat for about 10 minutes until soft. Add cumin and coriander and cook a further 3 minutes, then remove from the heat and add beetroot harissa, mint and coconut. Stir in eggs and cool.

Press coconut mix onto lamb racks to form a crust. Cover and chill for 30 minutes.

Place racks in a roasting pan and roast at 210°C for 20 minutes.

To make the harissa, blend the chillies with the paprika, garlic, coriander, caraway, cumin, salt and beetroot in a food processor. Add lemon juice and olive oil to make a thick paste. Pack into a jar and seal.

Serve with underground nut mixture.

*Underground nuts, or jungo beans, are indigenous and grow prolifically in certain areas of South Africa, especially KwaZulu-Natal. They have very hard outer shells and must be soaked before peeling.

'

All chefs should stand at the backdoor when the plates come back. This is a very valuable learning experience because it is there that we can see what the guests liked and disliked. This helps us to remember we are cooking for those who are ultimately paying our salaries.

,

granadilla and lime curd towers

Serves 4 – 6

Pastry
1 whole egg
1 yolk
90g icing sugar
zest of 1 lemon
100g soft butter
250g flour

Lime curd
50g butter
175g sugar
3 extra large eggs, beaten
4 limes, rind and juice
the pulp of 4 granadillas

Meringue
2 extra large egg whites
pinch salt
60ml castor sugar
60ml icing sugar, sifted

To make pastry, place egg, yolk, icing sugar and zest in a blender and process until combined. Add soft butter and combine. Add flour and process until just combined. Knead lightly until smooth. Cover and chill for at least 20 minutes. Roll out and line muffin pans. Chill for a further 10 minutes. Bake blind for 10–15 minutes at 200°C until golden. Remove from oven and cool to room temperature.

To make the curd, melt the butter, add sugar, eggs, lime juice and rind. Cook over a low heat in a double-boiler, stirring continuously until thick, which will take about 10–15 minutes. Cool to room temperature, fold in granadilla pulp and refrigerate.

Fill pastry bases with curd.

To make meringue, whip up the egg whites with salt until stiff. Fold in castor sugar, a little at a time, until thick, beating all the time. Fold in icing sugar. Place mixture in a piping bag and pipe a swirl on top of each curd.

Bake at 160°C for 10–15 minutes.

"In many poor cultures, the locals are eating what they can lay their hands on — survival food. Even then there is joy and celebration in sharing what little they have — it is their way of showing hospitality. Sitting around a communal platter sharing food in a communal style is a food experience like no other.

Evonne Short"

A decade as the Food Editor of *True Love* magazine took Dorah Sitole to the forefront of food development in South Africa. After numerous publications, including a number of cookbooks and radio and television shows, Dorah became a household name to many South African cooks.

It was Iris Grootboom – *the* caterer in Soweto in the seventies – who played the greatest role in laying the foundations of Dorah's career in food. As a novice newlywed she made food her hobby, attending cookery demonstrations and collecting recipes, all of which she pasted up in books. It was these books that convinced the Canned Food Advisory Service to employ her in a promotions capacity. There she learnt the foundations of her career in recipe development, cookery demonstrations, food writing and food styling.

Dorah Sitole

'

All the years that I have been involved in food, a good twenty years, I have been exploring and experimenting with food from all over the world. Now that I can concoct a croquembouche and flambé a crêpe suzette, I am struck by a strong craving for the food I grew up on ... or is it guilt? I am dabbling and experimenting with indigenous ingredients as never before, and I am amazed at the results! As one cook put it, 'The pleasures of cooking are bound with memories of our childhood.' When other cuisines were developing and taking their rightful places on the menus of the world, traditional food was relegated to 'survival food' status. Granted, a new urban cuisine did evolve which embraces and enhances all the flavours of African food. Even that, with all its exciting robust flavours, has not really made it onto the greater local food scene yet. However, in the townships and African suburban society circles, a celebration menu without traditional food is considered passé. At last culture food is slowly but surely becoming trendy.

,

umnqusho – samp & beans

This Xhosa recipe has become a popular traditional dish throughout the country. The original recipe uses only samp and beans, but modern cooks add various other kinds of interesting ingredients.

Serves 4–6

800g samp
400g dried beans – butter or sugar beans or a mix
3 litres water
4 chicken stock cubes
salt and pepper to taste
60ml margarine

Soak the samp and beans in water overnight. To cook, cover samp completely with water in a large saucepan and bring to the boil.
Add stock cubes, salt and pepper. Lower the heat and cook gently until samp is soft (approximately 2 hours). Replenish the water constantly as samp absorbs a lot of water while cooking. When the samp is cooked, add the margarine and mash well to mix.

Variations
All these variations can be added together to the samp for an exotic flavour:
Add 3 peeled, diced potatoes 30 minutes before end of cooking time and mash into the samp.
Add 125ml of instant milk powder to samp when mashing. For an interesting flavour, season with 30ml curry powder or masala mix. Sauté chopped onion, crushed garlic, crushed ginger and chopped green pepper together and mash into samp when adding margarine.

amanqina – pork trotters in wine

Trotters (lamb, pork or cow heels) and the head are served the day after a feast. Traditionally, the task of cleaning them (and sometimes feasting on them) is a function of the men. They are considered a delicacy as the numbers are limited. These days women also enjoy them and they can be prepared in all kinds of exotic ways.

Serves 4–6

1kg pork trotters, cleaned and sliced
60ml oil
2 onions, chopped
250g button mushrooms, chopped
1 packet cream of mushroom soup powder, dissolved in 125ml water
250ml dry red wine
salt and freshly ground black pepper to taste

Cook the trotters in salted water for 1½ hours or until tender.
Heat oil in a separate saucepan and sauté onion until transparent. Add mushrooms and continue cooking until onions are brown.
Stir in the mushroom soup, wine and seasoning. Bring to the boil, add cooked trotters and simmer gently for 20 minutes.
Serve on samp or with a dumpling.

phuthu
savoury crumbly pap

Considered to be a typical Zulu dish, phuthu pap has become a favourite in most homes. Sour milk 'amasi' is served and enjoyed with phuthu. It is also makes an interesting accompaniment to a braai, especially if you enhance the flavour with other ingredients. Due to its versatility and bland flavour, it also makes a good accompaniment to other foods.

Serves 4–6

125ml water
500ml mealie meal
60ml oil
1 onion, chopped
1 clove garlic, crushed
5ml turmeric
1 red or green sweet pepper, chopped
salt and pepper, to taste
45ml parmesan cheese, grated

To make the phutu bring the water to a slow boil and stir in the mealie meal. Stir continuously, using a fork, until the mixture becomes crumbly and cooked – approximately 15 minutes.
Heat oil and sauté onion and garlic until transparent. Add turmeric, sweet pepper, salt and pepper. Fry for 5 minutes.
Gently mix in phutu and parmesan cheese, then heat through for about 10 minutes.

inyama ye nkukhu
chicken yassa

Chicken slaughtered at home has a special flavour to it. Most butchers and street vendors in the township sell ready slaughtered chickens, which makes life easier. The yassa sauce is a West African recipe picked up on my African travels. It gives the chicken an unusual tangy flavour.

Serves 4–6

1 chicken, portioned (preferably slaughtered at home)
salt and pepper to taste
15ml mixed masala
oil

Yassa sauce
4 onions, sliced
75ml lemon juice
1 green chilli, chopped
500ml chicken stock
10ml mixed herbs

Season chicken pieces with salt, pepper and masala. Heat oil and fry chicken until brown.
Prepare marinade by heating remaining oil and frying onion until golden. Mix in remaining ingredients and cook for 5 minutes.
Add chicken, cover and allow to marinate for about 3 hours or overnight. Gently cook chicken in sauce for 1 hour or until tender.
Serve over savoury phuthu or rice.

amaphaphu
lamb lights in peanut sauce

Lamb lights (lungs) are also a delicacy eaten when there is a feast, together with tripe and other organs from the animal slaughtered for the occasion. The peanut sauce is undoubtedly Africa's favourite condiment, added to cooked mopani worms, dried morogo or dried meat.

Serves 4–6

1kg lamb lights (lungs)
60ml oil
1 onion, chopped
1 clove garlic, crushed
30ml ginger, crushed
1 green pepper, chopped
4 tomatoes, peeled and chopped
salt and pepper
5ml cayenne pepper
10ml curry powder
60ml peanut butter
250ml water

Cook lungs in salted water until tender. Remove and cut into bite-sized strips.
Heat oil and sauté onion, garlic, ginger and green pepper, until soft. Add tomatoes, seasoning, peanut butter and water. Bring to the boil and add lungs.
Simmer gently for about 20 minutes to blend flavours.
Serve with phuthu, samp dumpling or pap and spinach.

morogo
braised spinach

Wherever you go in Africa there is a wild leaf of some sort that is enjoyed by the locals. In South Africa we have 'morogo', a collective name for various wild leaves. With urbanisation it has become difficult to get the real thing and spinach has sucessfully taken over. There are numerous ways of preparing spinach, ranging from mixing it with tomato and onion relish, or mashing it with potatoes, peanut butter and onions, to adding exotic ingredients like cream, mushrooms and nutmeg. Beetroot leaves have also become a good substitute for morogo.

Serves 4

45ml butter
1 leek, sliced into strips
30ml crushed ginger
1 clove garlic, crushed
salt and freshly ground black pepper
5ml ground cumin
5ml ground coriander
3ml ground nutmeg
1 bunch baby spinach, washed and chopped
60ml toasted almonds, chopped (optional)

Melt butter and sauté leeks, ginger and garlic until soft. Season with salt, pepper and spices.
Add spinach, mix well and cook gently, stirring constantly until cooked through – approximately 20 minutes.
Serve sprinkled with nuts, if desired.

idombolo
steamed dumpling *(illustrated on p. 149)*

Idombolo should never be steamed over a stew. It is sometimes made with fermented porridge to give it a musty taste. This traditional bread is popular among all African tribes and each one has a special way of making it.

Serves 4–6

750ml flour
250ml maize meal
10g instant dry yeast
30ml sugar
5ml salt
1 egg, beaten
about 500ml lukewarm water or water mixed
*   with milk*

Sift flour and mix in maize meal, dry yeast, sugar and salt. Mix egg with water. Add enough lukewarm liquid to the dry ingredients to form a soft but pliable dough. Knead for 10 minutes. Cover dough with plastic and leave to rise until double in size. Knock dough down and place in a greased enamel bowl. Allow to rise once again until double in size before steaming.
Meanwhile prepare a pot for steaming. Bring water to the boil in a pot large enough to hold the bowl containing the dumpling. Immerse it in the hot water (the water should come one third of the way up the sides of the dish). Seal the pot tightly and simmer gently for 1 hour. Avoid opening the saucepan whilst steaming. Replenish water if necessary.
To serve, cut the dumpling into wedges.

<u>Variations</u>: To make herb dumpling add 30ml chopped parsley. For corn dumpling add 1 x 400g can whole kernel corn at the second kneading.

umqombothi
sorghum beer

Makes 10 litres

6kg mtombo (sorghum)
3kg mealie meal
5 litres boiling water
6 litres cold water

Mix 3kg sorghum with 3kg mealie meal, add 5 litres of boiling water, leave to cool, then stir in 1kg more of the sorghum. Allow to stand overnight. Place mixture in a large saucepan, add 3 litres of cold water and boil for 1 hour. Leave to cool.
Place mixture in a large bucket and add remaining 2kg sorghum. Add the rest of the cold water and mix well. Cover mixture with a piece of plastic or damp cloth and allow to stand for at least 12 hours to brew.
Using a large metal or conical basket sieve, strain mixture well, making sure that all the liquid is pressed out.
Serve cold.

"

I most certainly feel that we are blessed to be such a cosmopolitan nation. We are exposed to so many culinary styles, all of which are important parts of the kaleidoscope. One wonders, though, if there will be a fair balance in this 'fusion food'. Will the more acceptable foods dominate this 'rainbow cuisine', and those that are a bit threatening or unknown not even make an appearance? I believe a perfect setting already exists: urban African, Cape Malay and boerekos, side-by-side and unadulterated, are typical and unique to our nation. Other cuisines are there for us to enjoy and to celebrate our diversity.

Dorah Sitole

'

Arnold Ta

As a Dutch national who grew up in South Africa, Tanzer elected to do his chef's training in The Netherlands. His first job was in a Mexican restaurant, after which he landed a job working under Michelin star chef Robert Kranenborg. The five-year apprenticeship in classical French cooking he received here was the best foundation in food he could have asked for.

Seeking adventure, Tanzer travelled the world – from movie sets to exclusive kitchens – as personal chef to actor Michael Douglas. On his return to Africa, he joined the Conservation Corporation Africa, with its lodges and bush camps throughout he continent. It was during this time that the idea of his very own company, Outta the Blue Solutions, came to him and his partner Lisa Pearse. This partnership enables them to offer a complete package to the hospitality industry, from a housekeeping and accommodation service to food and training.

Arnold Tanzer

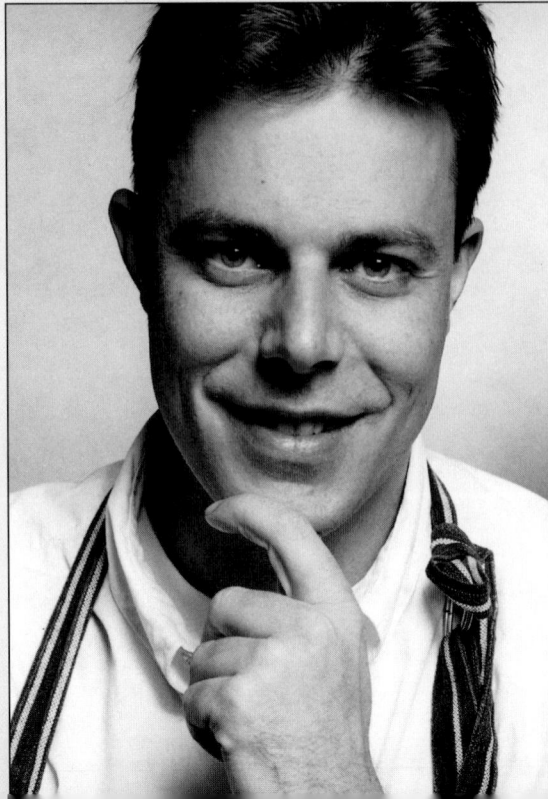

'

South Africa is a country rich in eclectic cuisine and culture, yet most restaurants and hotels are bogged in the legacy of our colonial past, with overcooked beef, heavy 'grey' white sauce, soggy boiled vegetables and cooked sweet puddings. Very few reflect the zestful, delectable blend of flavours and smells born from a mosaic of culture and tradition.

A favourite pastime is to spend the morning coursing the local markets, such as the Oriental Plaza, downtown Diagonal Street and Chinatown, unearthing ingredients and flavours used by the ordinary people from diverse backgrounds – Indian, African, Chinese, English, Dutch, Portuguese. The treasures discovered – tamarind pods, Chinese long beans, lemon grass, luvu beans, green mangoes, madumbe, morogo – united with ordinary produce such as chicken, beef, fresh fish, vegetables, create an elaborate modern cuisine that reflects our country.

Ingredients are flash fried, dried, preserved, pickled, salted, smoked, grilled, charred, steamed, mashed, marinated, basted, slow cooked, pot roasted, sautéed and even buried in sand to achieve the required effect. Traditional tastes and techniques are played with in this marriage to achieve a sense of balance and to explore the tastes from this vast ever-changing continent in all its diverse forms. An Anglo bread and butter pudding is cooked over the coals to achieve a smoky taste and then smothered with sweet orange blossom custard. Samp and beans are cooked in chicken stock, then drizzled with a fruity olive oil, scattered with fresh basil and finally topped with fresh spicy garlicky prawns.

,

African mezze platter

eggplants with chilli

1kg baby eggplant
salt
30ml olive oil
3 cloves of garlic,
2 chillies, chopped
60ml lemon juice
flat-leaf parsley to serve

Pierce each eggplant with a knife a couple of times and then sprinkle with salt. Stand for about 30 minutes to disgorge, then brush with olive oil. Roast at 180°C for 20 minutes or until soft. Heat olive oil, add garlic, chopped chillies (remove the seeds for a less intense flavour) and lemon juice. Marinate eggplant in liquid for 30 minutes. To serve, sprinkle with flat-leaf parsley.

spicy pumpkin and cumin dip

6 cups pumpkin, peeled and cubed
vegetable stock
30ml cumin seeds
3 garlic cloves
seeds of 1 small red bird's eye chilli
lemon juice
seasoning

Boil pumpkin until tender in a vegetable stock. Toast cumin seeds. Drain pumpkin, add cumin, garlic cloves and chilli seeds. Blend until smooth, adding lemon juice and seasoning to taste.

roasted pepper and tomato relish

3 large red sweet peppers
olive oil
1 large red onion, sliced
3 garlic cloves
5ml turmeric
6 large tomatoes, peeled and quartered
fresh coriander
mint

Coat red peppers with olive oil and roast at 180°C until the skin blisters. Place peppers in a sealed plastic container until they have reached room temperature. Peel off the skin and remove seeds. Slice onion and sauté with garlic cloves and turmeric until tender, but not brown. Chop peppers and add tomatoes. Sauté for about 5 minutes in a frying pan and then sprinkle with fresh coriander and mint.

grilled madumbe* with ginger dressing

500g madumbes
olive oil
sea salt
cracked black pepper.
10ml garlic, minced
10ml ginger, mincedc
lime zest

Peel and slice madumbes, then blanch in salted water. Heat a griddle, brush madumbe slices with olive oil and grill until brown. Season with sea salt and black pepper. To make the dressing, whisk together garlic and ginger with lime zest and olive oil. Drizzle over madumbe.
*Madumbes are an indigenous root to be treated like potatoes.

smoked chicken, luvu nuts and dried apricots

1 smoked chicken breast
salt and cracked pepper
*200g luvu nuts**
80g apricots
fresh coriander or fenugreek, finely chopped
olive oil

Shred chicken breast and season with salt and cracked pepper. Boil and peel luvu nuts and add to chicken. Chop the apricots and toss into chicken. Add coriander or fenugreek. Drizzle with olive oil.
*Luvu nuts are found in KwaZulu-Natal.

*In Africa nothing is wasted, there must be food for everyone.
African people sit to enjoy a meal in a group. This culture is
central to their existence.*

blackened beef with saffron mayonnaise

Serves 4

*2 garlic cloves, crushed
15ml fresh ginger
3 chillies
10ml fenugreek seeds
5ml turmeric
5ml ground coriander
1 small onion
1 small beef fillet*

Saffron mayonnaise
*250ml olive oil
1 egg yolk
10ml lime juice
1 pinch saffron threads
10ml hot water
fine sea salt*

Make a paste with garlic, ginger and chillies.
Add fenugreek seeds and turmeric. Blend in
coriander and onion. Season the fillet with this
spice paste and leave to stand for 2 hours.
To make the saffron mayonnaise, whisk olive oil
into egg yolk drop by drop, then add lime juice.
Keep whisking until a thick homogenous mixture has formed.
Heat saffron threads in hot water. Blend into
mayonnaise and season with fine sea salt.
Roast beef fillet over a high heat on a griddle
pan or over the braai until medium-rare (or as
desired).
Serve with mayonnaise and fresh green salad.

'

I like strong flavour in food and Africa reflects that. Eating is all about taste and textures. Roast, grilled, poached, crunch, drizzle help to make it a complete experience.

'

pot roasted guinea fowl with cinnamon

served with preserved lemons and pomegranate seeds

Serves 4

guinea fowl
flour
10ml cinnamon
15ml soya sauce
zest of 2 lemons
25ml olive oil
15ml ginger
2 garlic cloves, crushed
salt & pepper
15ml runny honey
4 large onions, chopped
coarsely ground black pepper
2–3 preserved lemons*
500ml chicken stock
seeds of 1 fresh pomegranate or dried
   seeds**
45ml fresh coriander, chopped

Dust the guinea fowl with flour. Season with cinnamon, soya sauce and lemon zest
Heat olive oil and sauté ginger in a large pot with a lid. Add garlic, then brown the fowl. Add remaining seasoning and runny honey.
Add onions to the pot. Scatter in coarsely ground black pepper and the preserved lemons. Add chicken stock, cover and simmer for 1 hour. Just before serving add the pomegranate seeds and fresh coriander.

*Preserved lemons are a Moroccan original. They are sliced, packed in salt and stored for 3–4 weeks then sealed in a preserving jar. They are found at speciality stores.
**Dried pomegranate seeds can be obtained from speciality spice stores.

'

Just because something like warthog is braaied, served with mealie meal and cooked in a boma doesn't make it traditionally African.

,

poached prickly pears with fresh cheese

Serves 4

8 prickly pears, peeled
250ml red wine
100g sugar
1 cinnamon stick
5 cloves

Fresh cheese
2 limes, grated zest & juice
50g sugar
2ml cumin
250g fresh mascarpone cheese

Peel prickly pears carefully, using a fork to hold them steady. Slice off ends and make an incision lengthwise, then run a knife underneath and prise back the skin.
Boil red wine with sugar, cinnamon stick and cloves. Add the prickly pears and gently simmer until soft.
To make the cheese, whisk the lime zests and juice together with sugar and cumin into fresh mascarpone cheese.
Hang in a muslin cloth in the fridge for two days, so that the whey can drain off.
Serve a spoonful of cheese with the prickly pears and poaching sauce.

'

We need to delve into our diverse cultures and give expression to a cuisine that reflects the fiery chilli bright soul of Africa combined with the cucumber cool of a modern democratic state, yet retains the cappuccino earthiness of its people.

Arnold Tanzer

'